From the Lips of Children

From the Lips of Children

Richard Wurmbrand

HODDER AND STOUGHTON
·LONDON SYDNEY AUCKLAND TORONTO

Illustrations by Peter S. Smith

British Library Cataloguing in Publication Data

Wurmbrand, Richard
  From the lips of children.—(Hodder
  Christian paperbacks)
  1. Children—Religious life
  2. Christian life
  I. Title
  248.8'2   BV4571.2

ISBN 0 340 39267 3

'To lovely Rosemary Harris, a loving friend with a child's heart, the first to introduce me to churches in Britain'

Contents

A ship's captain took his six-year-old daughter with him on an ocean journey. A terrible storm arose, and the order was given for everybody to enter the lifeboats.

A maid came into the captain's cabin, where his little girl was sleeping, and woke her. 'Quick! Come with me! The ship is sinking.'

The girl asked, 'Where is my father?'

'The captain is at the helm.'

'Then,' said the girl calmly, 'I can go back to sleep. He will not let the ship sink when his child is on board.'

*   *   *

A child, standing on the ocean shore, waved to an ocean liner passing by, hailing the captain to take him on board. An adult watching him in amusement finally spoke. 'Don't be silly! You can hitchhike by car, but not by ocean liner!'

Undaunted, the boy continued to signal. Suddenly a boat was lowered from the ship. Sailors came to the shore to pick the boy up. As they left he shouted back to the astonished observer, 'You see – I wasn't silly. I knew what I was doing. The captain of the ship is my father!'

*   *   *

May we have such childlike trust in our Captain!

Acknowledgments

Almost all the sayings of children recorded in this book have been gathered by myself at the very source – 'from the lips of children'. However, I acknowledge gratefully other sources, including Alfonse de Liguori's *Life of Martyrs* (for stories of children who died for Christ); the secretly printed magazines of the Soviet underground churches (for stories of prisoners' children); various Christian publications including *Daily Bread* and *Portals of Prayer*, and a few foreign publications.

Some of these stories have appeared in several versions in various places. It has sometimes been impossible to find the original source.

Where I quote from children's own remarks, I have used only their words. I hope they will not insist on their copyright! Almost all the commentaries are my own.

Richard Wurmbrand

Prologue

"Jesus is going to come back with his arms full of toys."

Today new theologies are sweeping, like weather fronts, across the globe: black theology, God-is-dead theology, feminist theology, liberation theology, and many more.

So why should we introduce yet another – 'children's theology'?

Jesus would surely have preferred it to some other human fabrications. In fact He endorsed it: 'I tell you the truth, unless you change and become like little children, you will never enter the kingdom of heaven' (Matt. 18:3).

To become like little children means to think as they do, and that is as true in theological matters as in any other. My grandson Alex (who at six years old was quite well read in the Scriptures) once said to me, 'The Bible is meant for children. Only the Children of Israel came out of slavery in Egypt; the grown-ups stayed behind. Only the Children of God enter heaven. It will be a country without any grown-ups!'

Little did he know how close he was to the truth!

Jesus' teaching that we must become like little children has been the subject of much thought and discussion both by theologians and by philosophers. What exactly does Jesus mean? Does He mean that we have to become less complicated, more humble, more open, more trusting? Perhaps He means we must be prepared to play? What precisely are the characteristics of children which we are to imitate?

The German philosopher, Karl Jaspers, commented: 'It is part of the very essence of man that he is a philosopher, and there is a wonderful confirmation of that in the questions that children ask. It is not unusual to hear, from their lips, profoundly philosophical statements.'

The psychologist Carl Jung went even further. He suggested that adults whose minds were troubled should play with toys, like children. He himself, he said, had found it to be a helpful spiritual exercise.

A little Turkish girl of four years old, called Ariel, told me, 'Jesus is going to come back with his arms full of toys. He will even bring a piano for me!'

If we have not 'become like little children', to whom will Jesus give his playthings?

In the Bible it is written that 'a little child shall lead them' (Isa. 11:6). A child whose parents were divorced came across that verse and demanded, 'Then why don't they let us lead? We would never have invented pubs, casinos or nuclear war. If we were the leaders, there would be no spankings and no divorce.'

Jesus tells us that we must be born again, and that suggests that we must return to the innocence and trustfulness of childhood. But it must be a genuine return. We must not be people who put on childlikeness to order, but people who are childlike by nature, having a spontaneous sense of dependency and an awareness that we need to be guided.

Children have a great advantage; their minds are not compartmentalised. They do not make a distinction between the concrete and the abstract. They have no need to pretend.

So their thoughts on theological matters are of special interest to us.

I have often been taken aback by the remarkable insights of the children I have known. For many years now I have been recording their questions and comments, observations and insights. Many are from my own family, from my son Mihai and my grandchildren Amelie and Alex.

My hope is that the incidents which are recounted in this book will help you to listen the more perceptively to the children in your own life, and enable you to recapture some of the unsophisticated candour and openness that belong uniquely to childhood.

It is said that the child is father to the man. Similarly, a child's intuitions about God may well help adults to embrace true theology.

Beliefs

"It is cold outside. How are you?"

When he was five years old my son Mihai became dangerously ill. His life was threatened; he needed an emergency operation, a trepanning of the skull. This is a major operation, in which a piece of bone is removed to relieve pressure on the brain.

The night before the operation we called a number of fellow-believers to gather round his bed to pray for a successful outcome.

As I sat beside him I touched his body. It was burning with fever. I said to him, 'Tomorrow you are to have an operation, a dangerous one. It's possible that you will die.'

Mihai replied joyfully. 'Then I'll go to heaven! Angels must have splendid toys. An angel might teach me how to play the harp!'

'Well, it's not that simple; you are a sinner.'

'But Father, didn't you tell me that Jesus' blood cleanses us from sin? I'm not worried – I will be in heaven.'

'Well, Mihai, these brothers and sisters have come to pray for your welfare. The Bible says that when someone is sick, the elders of the Church should be called and they should pray over him. Then he will recover. Do you believe that?'

'I believe everything the Bible says,' he answered simply.

One brother after another prayed. Then Mihai himself prayed: 'I thank you, God, that you are making me healthy now, and that I will soon be able to go with my father to the toyshop to buy a new toy.'

My hand still lay on his chest. As he prayed I felt the fever diminish markedly. When he had finished his brief prayer, I said to my wife 'Take his temperature. God's miracles are measured with the thermometer!'

Sure enough, Mihai's temperature had dropped. There was no need of any operation the next day. Instead, he played in the garden.

Several days later, I was able to take him to the toy shop. At that time, the Soviet army had just invaded Rumania, our homeland, and had shown a marked liking for alcohol. A great deal of drunkenness was in evidence.

When we entered the department store, a Soviet captain was there with a woman sergeant. They were attempting to make some purchases, but were handicapped by not knowing our language. On the other hand, the salesman could not speak Russian. I offered to translate for them.

Mihai repeatedly urged me to tell them about Christ. I too was waiting for the right moment.

After I had helped them in their spending spree, the sergeant said to me, 'You have been so kind to us.

Perhaps you could do me one more favour. I need some dresses. Where can I find them?'

Now I knew she was at my mercy!

'I haven't the slightest idea about such matters – but may I invite the captain and you to come to our home for lunch? Afterwards, my wife will take you shopping.'

Mihai was delighted that we would have them in our home, where they could learn about the faith. 'Buy them a bottle of wine,' he urged. 'Then they'll listen better. You know that all their soldiers are drunkards!'

Probably he had heard me quote Paul's words: 'To the Jews I became like a Jew, to win the Jews. . . . To the weak I became weak, to win the weak' (1 Cor. 9:20, 22). I smiled at his ingenuous suggestion; but I was indeed able to share with my guests the fruit of the True Vine, which gives life eternal.

Both officers were converted.

*   *   *

In the Soviet Union, Piotr, whose father was in prison for his faith, was interrogated at school by a police officer who had a hidden motive for his questions. Smiling and apparently sympathetic, the officer said, 'I really like your father, and I want him released. But I need more information about him. Tell me about your father.'

'Oh!' replied Piotr. 'He tells beautiful children's stories. When he speaks it's as if Jesus were present in the room. Only last Christmas he told us how Jesus was born in a manger, and how wise men came to worship Him. We should worship Him, too.'

The officer ignored this. 'Where was this gathering? Who was present? Who else spoke?'

The child sensed the danger. 'I can tell you the whole story just as my father told it. Beyond that I have nothing to say to you. You are not one of our people. I don't trust you.'

Many disasters have been caused in the Church by unveiling its mysteries to the profane, and by casting the pearls of the Kingdom before swine. It is important to cultivate a discerning spirit, such as Piotr had.

* * *

When young Alex arrived home from holiday with his parents, he went round the house kissing the front door, his pillow, and many other things, repeating 'This is my home.'

We should have that same spirit as we approach the heavenly Jerusalem, which is our everlasting home. Even though we may live very comfortably here, we are still pilgrims and strangers in this world.

A missionary came back to the United States after forty years of service in Africa, where he had endured many hardships. Sailing on the same ship was President Theodore Roosevelt, returning from an elephant-hunting safari.

A large crowd turned out to greet the president, but no one came to meet the missionary. He was feeling very sorry for himself. Then he was comforted by an inner voice that reminded him: 'The president has come home; you are not home yet.'

When we reach the heavenly Jerusalem, we too will impulsively kiss the door and threshold of our real home.

* * *

Here are some letters written to Basil Rishuk, imprisoned in the USSR for his Christian faith, by his children Andrew (ten years old), Gena (twelve), and Tanya (fourteen).

I kiss you, dear Daddy, in the love of Christ. As I write, it is cold and unpleasant outside. How are you? How is your health? May the Lord shed in our hearts the peace and joy that Jesus gives, in spite of all the tempests. We will always trust only in Him. We believe that He will give us power for the fight, that He will help us to withstand the tempest.

It is important to withstand it, because we know that the calm follows the storm and that this time it will be eternal, with a happiness that has no end.

At home, everything is going well. We live in the hope of seeing you, but also of seeing the Lord, so that we may enter into eternal life, where no one will separate us.

A hearty kiss.

Your son, Andrew.

Dear Daddy, I greet you in the love of our Lord Jesus Christ. Papa, we never forget you. We pray constantly to God for you. We pray for your health. We pray also for all prisoners, and trust that God will keep them.

Daddy, ask the prison commander to allow a personal visit, for it is a long time until the New Year and we all want to come to you. We have such a yearning for you!

Your loving son, Gena.

Dear Daddy, Christ has risen!

How are you? May the resurrected Lord illumine your camp, so that you may be joyous even in sorrow. When I hear hymns sung my heart shrinks and tears run, though I screw my eyes up as tight as I can. May we see each other soon. You are alone, and we are all together. But soon all will pass, and then you will be with us.

Be strong.

Your daughter, Tanya.

May we learn from such children to have a burning love for our imprisoned brothers and sisters in Christ.

* * *

A Methodist missionary in Africa told of a child who went to Sunday School and there heard the story of Abel sacrificing a lamb to God.

The next day the child made an altar from a few stones out on the fields. On it, he placed a mutton chop. Then he prayed.

'O God, my Father, I have made You a sacrifice. I have only two pence, so I can't buy a lamb. If I owned any lambs I would give You one; but I only have this meat. Please, my Father, send fire down from heaven to consume it.'

God did touch the meat, though not with fire. Ants consumed it. Ants belong to God just as much as a flame of fire does.

May we have a child's readiness to follow the example of the saints of old, and bring sacrifices to God.

*   *   *

It might seem that the ultimate anguish is to lose a child through death.

It is not so. There is worse suffering.

In the village of Dubrovo in the Soviet Union, a family named Sloboda (the name means 'liberty' in Russian) had committed the crime of being Christians.

For that crime Mrs. Sloboda was jailed for four years. Her five children – Galia, Shura, Kolia, Liusa, Pavlik (the youngest five years old) – were taken away and placed in an atheistic children's camp.

This type of separation is more difficult to bear than that of death. Mrs. Sloboda never saw her children again. At the age of forty-nine she died in prison, as a result of torture. The children were only allowed to attend her burial. At her grave, they recited this prayer: 'Lord, our mother has died. Help us to be as righteous as she has been. Help us to give a witness such as she has given. Amen.'

And that was all. Unafraid of pain, they had decided to walk the way of martyrdom. Detention in the Communist camp had neither frightened nor 're-educated' them.

Accepting suffering for Christ's sake will be an essential part of children's theology, if they are provided with true Christian models.

* * *

In Communist Rumania, a Christian girl named Viorica was beaten harshly in school because she had invited her schoolmates to church. She fainted during the beating, and an ambulance had to take her to hospital.

Two days passed before she regained consciousness. When she did, the doctor at her bedside said, 'You poor girl, at last you have opened your eyes. All this time I have been thinking of the cruelty of the Director who beat you like this. My heart has been bitter with hatred. I wish I could take revenge on him.'

Viorica smiled. 'There is no need to hate him. Jesus taught us to love everyone. Just before I opened my eyes, I saw Him and talked to Him. He asked me whether it still hurt. And He told me that in heaven I will receive a very beautiful crown, which is reserved only for those who have suffered for Him. He told me to pray for those who mistreated me, and to love them, because our influence will help them to give their lives to God and so become His children.'

According to children's theology, this is how a Christian should react to being flogged. Like their Saviour, they know how to love when abused, and how to forgive when persecuted.

* * *

Charles Spurgeon once said, 'A child of five, if properly instructed, can as truly believe and be regenerated as an adult.' This suggests that a child so instructed can have very valuable theological insights.

When he was a child Spurgeon's mother told him, 'Charles, your father and I have trained you in righteousness. We have taught you the Word of God. We have lived a godly life before you. If you do not live a godly life, we will stand before God in the day of judgement and bear witness against you.'

A friend once argued with the adult Spurgeon that children cannot really understand the gospel. Spurgeon took him to his Sunday School, where the gentleman asked one of the boys, 'What kind of a heart do you have?'

'A very good one, sir,' was the reply.

The man turned to Spurgeon. 'You see? He does not understand the ABC of the gospel. He does not realise that he is a sinner.'

Spurgeon asked the child, 'How do you know your heart is good?'

'Well,' he answered, 'I had an old heart, inherited from my ancestors who were sinners. But Jesus gave me a new heart. Jesus has no bad hearts to give! If He gave me a heart I am sure it is an excellent one.'

*   *   *

Heinrich Heine, the German Jewish-Christian poet who lived in the first part of the nineteenth century, wrote of his early yearnings for God:

As a little child I was already asking questions such as, Who is God? and, What does He look like? I could spend whole days looking up towards heaven and would be very sad in the evening because I had not seen the most holy face of God, but only grey, silly caricatures formed of clouds. I was totally confused by astronomical events, which were not concealed even from little children, and constantly marvelled that these thousand million stars were big, beautiful earth-balls like ours and that one single God ruled over each shining world.

I remember that once, in a dream, I saw God very high up and far away. He looked happily through a little window in heaven, with the face of a pious old man with a small Jewish beard, and scattered downward a multitude of seeds that blossomed as they fell from heaven, grew in the infinity of space, and enlarged until they became glittering, populated worlds, each as big as our earth.

I could never forget this vision. Several times I saw the happy old man, sowing the seeds of worlds from His small window in heaven. Once I heard Him click His tongue as our maid did when she threw barley to the chickens.[1]

As an adult Heine mocked religion and the churches. He became the great friend of Karl Marx, the God-hater, and forgot this vision, which became a reality to him again only a short time before his death.

Those who are privileged to know God when they are children should strive to retain their tender images of Him, and not surrender them to pseudo-intellectualism. 'Remember your first love,' says Jesus. (If we fail to do so, the images of those early days may come back to haunt us at death.)

* * *

When she was four years old, Amelie was alone with my wife and me in the chapel of Campus Crusade in San Bernadino, California.

Suddenly, without any prompting, she stepped forward and said: 'Jesus, I am Yours.'

Since that time she has steadfastly resisted any calls to commit herself to Christ. 'I did so once,' she says. 'I am a child of God. I'm sure of it.'

If a child can be so sure that Christ has received her into His loving care, why should we ever doubt that He has accepted us, as our Saviour?

* * *

---

1. Heinrich Heine, *Works* (Lowit, Germany), Vol. II, pp. 425–56.

Julieta was an aristocratic lady who lived during the reign of the fourth-century Roman emperor, the cruel Diocletian.

She was asked to bring a sacrifice to a heathen altar, but answered, 'I am a Christian. I am prepared to lose not only my property but even my life, rather than deny my God.'

Alexander, proconsul of Cilicia, ordered that Julieta's three-year-old child Quiricus be torn from her embrace and be flogged to a pulp.

The child saw his mother's agony and struggled to return to her. But he was held back by Alexander, who sat him on his knees and tried to kiss him. Punching and kicking, Quiricus freed himself from the tyrant and cried out, 'I too am a Christian!'

In a rage Alexander grabbed him and beat him to death. The ground was spattered with the boy's blood and brains. Julieta, who was herself being flogged, cried 'I give You thanks, O my God, because You have called my boy to Yourself before me.'

Would we have the courage to say, 'I too am a Christian,' if it meant 'I too am prepared to die under torture for Christ'?

A child did so.

* * *

St. Cyril, who was born at Caesarea, became a Christian while he was a child. In consequence he was ill-treated, and finally turned out of his home, by his idolatrous father.

Word of this reached the judge, who summoned Cyril to appear before him. He had been told that the child frequently called upon the name of Jesus. So he promised Cyril that he would work out a reconciliation between him and his father – on condition that he promised never to utter that name again.

The child answered: 'I am content to be turned out of my father's house, because I shall receive a more spacious mansion in heaven. Neither do I fear death; by dying, I shall obtain a better life.'

In order to frighten him the judge ordered him to be bound and had him led away, apparently to execution. But he secretly gave orders that the boy should not be harmed. The executioner brought Cyril to a blazing fire and threatened to throw him in. But Cyril was quite prepared to lose his life.

The executioner then brought him back to the judge, who said to him, 'My child, you saw the fire. Cease to be a Christian, so that you can go back to your father's house and inherit your estates.'

Cyril replied: 'I fear neither fire nor sword. But I long to have a dwelling more magnificent, and riches that will last longer, than my father's. God will accept me. So hasten to put me to death, so that I can quickly go to enjoy Him.'

Those standing by wept, to hear the child speak in this way.

'You must not weep,' said Cyril, 'but rather rejoice, and encourage me in my suffering, so that I may come to have that house which I desire so passionately.'

He did not flinch from his position, and when death came he suffered it with joy.

*   *   *

In the sixteenth century there was a great persecution of Christians in Japan, under the Emperor Taicosoma.

At first, the officers whose responsibility it was to make up the list of Christians to be executed refused to include the name of little Louis. But the boy, who had been baptised only a few days earlier, cried and begged to have his name on the list. Eventually he was successful.

As he was led to his death, which was to be by crucifixion, his face radiated joyful confidence; and those who were watching were deeply moved.

The under-governor of Nagasaki presided over the execution. He was willing to release Louis, provided that he was prepared to renounce the Christian religion. But the child declared, 'On such a condition I do not want to live. If I die, I shall be losing this short and miserable life and gaining a happy and eternal one.'

When he saw the cross, upon which he was to be nailed, he ran to embrace it. The cross had always been an object very dear to him.

*   *   *

In another Japanese province, there was a further persecution of Christians a century later under King Canzugedono. Another little Louis was condemned to die, and his mother with him. His last words to her were, 'My dear mother, I will not forget to call upon the name of Jesus as long as I am alive.'

They bound him to a small cross, opposite his mother, and he continually repeated the sacred name. His executioner, in a fury, killed him with his lance.

Let us learn from such children to find, in the very name of Jesus, comfort in all suffering.

*   *   *

On that occasion, two more children were sentenced to death: Thomas, who was twelve years old, and Peter who was only six.

Their fathers were sentenced first. When Thomas heard that his father was to be a martyr, he longed so passionately for such a death for himself that when his own turn came he hastened to join him. Embracing his father, he said, 'I am going to die with you for the faith. We will go to heaven together.'

The executioner wanted to spare Thomas the horror of seeing his father being tortured, but the child cried out, 'I want to die with him!' They brought him near to where the bleeding body lay. There, his face radiant, he offered his head to the executioner.

Little Peter also said, of his father, 'They will make me die with him because I am a Christian. And I am so glad!'

Arriving at the place of execution, he knelt readily. Seeing the executioner with his sword, he extended his neck, all the time clasping his hands in prayer.

The executioner was deeply moved, and he replaced his sword in its scabbard. 'I have no heart to kill this innocent lamb,' he protested. A second executioner did likewise, and so did a third. The child knelt patiently until a fourth executioner carried out the sentence.

* * *

Those who are now past childhood, but have learned to become like children, think as these young martyrs thought.

Madame Guyon was a seventeenth-century contemplative who was imprisoned for several years because of her beliefs. 'I claim for my dowry,' she wrote, 'only crosses, scourges, persecutions, ignominies, lowliness, and nothingness of self; which God, in His goodness and wise purposes, grants unto me.'

Questions

"How can God think about me when He is busy with all the things He has to do in the world?"

Sometimes the thoughts of children explore unknown worlds.

'Do boys have boy angels, and girls have girl angels?' asked my granddaughter Amelie.

It was not a ridiculous question. Spiritual beings are not sexless. The 'great and wondrous sign' that John saw in his vision was no asexual being, but a woman (Rev. 12:1). Zechariah in his vision also saw women, some of them demonic (Zech. 5:7–9). The 'night creature' mentioned in Isaiah 34:14 (called, in Hebrew, *Lilith*) is believed in Jewish demonology to be the chief female wicked spirit.

* * *

Amelie asked her father, 'Why is it that your wishes are always the ones that have to be obeyed? The Constitution says that we have equal rights.'

It is a fair question. There is an answer to it. The Bible teaches great respect for one's parents. The only one of the Ten Commandments that promises a blessing is the fifth: 'Honour your father and your mother.' It is in the interest of children to be obedient: they get blessed.

Christian parents owe it to their children to give them this explanation. In fact, they should be ready to reply to any questions that their children ask, however uncomfortable.

For example, Amelie once asked, 'How was God the Father born? How did the whole thing begin? How did He come to be in heaven?'

The best answer is simply this: 'Whatever age we live to, we can only ever know a little. We must learn to accept that limitation, however old or young we may be.'

Moses warned, 'The secret things belong to the Lord our God: but the things revealed belong to us and to our children for ever' (Deut. 29:29). And on the last evening before His crucifixion, Jesus said to His disciples, 'I have much more to say to you, more than you can now bear' (John 16:12).

* * *

A question children often ask is, 'What does God look like?'

I have a simple answer: 'What does the image in a kaleidoscope look like?'

The image changes all the time.

In the Bible, God is likened to many things: love, a consuming fire, a lion, a stone, a man of war, the Ancient of Days, and many more. Everything can be in His image, because He encompasses everything. He is all in all.

If a child responds to this by saying, 'I can't understand,' then you must reply 'Neither can I'! God is not to be understood but to be ardently loved. He is beyond anything that man can imagine. He is what He is, not what we fancy Him to be.

*   *   *

'How can God think about me,' asked a child, 'when He is busy with all the things that He has to do in the world?'

Yet even man, with all his cares and activity, still has time to think about sub-microscopic atoms, even tinier electrons, and beyond them, the most miniscule elementary subparticles. He makes hypotheses about particles which he can only visualise mathematically, and builds vast nuclear chambers to isolate them, to prove their existence, because they constitute the very life of mankind and the essence of his environment.

We may be just as minuscule in the scheme of things, but we are very important to God; we are part of His inner life. 'In Him we live and move and have our being' (Acts 17:28).

God is as interested in us as we are interested in every facet of our bodies. Our minds are a part of His consciousness. God also cares about the most minute details of His creatures' lives.

A small boy asked his mother, 'Did God remember that you liked curly hair when He planned me?'

The answer is, 'Yes, He did.'

Another child wanted to know, 'Why did God make people, when He had the stars and the flowers?'

The answer is that it was for the same reason that we appreciate having brains as well as kidneys, lungs and toes – for the same reason that a man is not satisfied with a 'Mona Lisa' or a 'Venus de Milo', but prefers a woman who is alive, even though she may not possess an ideal beauty.

* * *

When I am out driving with my son and grandchildren, I often hear the familiar request, 'Grandpa, tell me a story!' And Amelie fastens the seat-belt, settles herself comfortably, and looks up at me expectantly.

On one occasion I decided to tell her about Noah's ark. But I had not been telling the story long when she interrupted.

'Why didn't the wolf eat the sheep in the ark?'

My son exchanged glances with me in the rear-view mirror. We took deep breaths and in turn tried to provide an answer. But Amelie was not satisfied. Then she brightened, and came up with an answer unassailable in its logic.

'I know! When each animal entered the ark, Noah fastened its seat-belt! He separated the wolf and the sheep, so the wolf could only snap and not bite.'

Perhaps Amelie was wiser than she knew. We would be well advised to widely separate individuals whose temperaments clash, and who generate quarrels and dissension when they are near to each other.

* * *

A child listened to a learned sermon that attempted to explain away the plain meaning of Scripture. Eventually she interrupted, exclaiming, 'If God did not mean what He said, why didn't he say what He did mean?'

Out of the mouth of babes!

* * *

When he was quite a small boy, Mihai asked, 'Why didn't God simply kill the devil, and put an end to all the trouble?' (When he was grown up, his own daughter Amelie asked exactly the same question.)

I replied, 'The devil was not always the devil. Once he

was a good angel, until the day came when he chose to become evil. If he had been killed, another good angel might have made the same choice. So killing the devil would have achieved nothing. Jesus did not say to the devil, "Perish!" He said, "Get behind me!" He puts demons to flight; He does not destroy them. We must develop that inner resistance. We must learn to do as Jesus did, and say to the devil, "No, I'm not going to listen to what you are suggesting."'

In his childish way, Mihai understood the point, and so in her turn did eight-year-old Amelie.

*   *   *

The famous American evangelist Billy Sunday told the story of a twelve-year-old boy who went to a preacher and begged him, 'Please go to the jail and speak to my Daddy. He murdered my Mummy. We loved him so much, he was always kind to us; but then he began to drink. It was whisky that made him do it. Now I have to look after my three small sisters. Please pray with him. He's going to be hanged tomorrow.'

He added, 'They told us we would be given his body. What am I going to do with it? Why don't they deliver it to the owner of the saloon that sold my father the whisky? Why don't they hang him? He murdered my father's soul before my father strangled my mother.'

Who is going to answer the questions children ask? Why is it that the people who receive the harsh punishments are those who commit the crimes, and not the brewers and publicans, the authors and publishers of obscene literature, and the producers of television shows that glorify violence – all of whom must share responsibility for incitement to crime? Why not indict those legislators and judges who let the poisoning of souls and minds go unpunished?

I can name very precisely those people who destroyed my soul with the poisonous ideas that they purveyed, when I was very young and lacked discernment. I also remember with shame that I too led others astray.

*   *   *

A child wanted to know, 'Will God do anything I ask Him to do? That is what He promised – can I rely on it? Can I really ask Him for anything at all?'

Yes, it is an all-embracing promise. 'Ask whatever you wish, and it will be given you,' says Jesus (John 15:7). But there is an 'if' preceding the promise: 'If you abide in me, and my words abide in you.'

Be a living part of the mystical body of Christ; let His words be your guide; and then you can ask anything, and you will have it.

Those who fulfil the condition will never ask for anything wrong.

*   *   *

Many children are still very young when it occurs to them to ask why there is so much evil in the world. But if they retain the mind of a child as they grow older, one can teach them to see good in everything, and potential good in everyone.

If a child asks, 'Why should there be evil?' then the answer must be, 'How can what we regard as evil be used for good?'

The crucifixion of Jesus was a terrible evil. But it served the greatest good that this world has ever known; the salvation of mankind.

*   *   *

The evangelist, Cerullo, asked a boy in Haiti: 'Do you know Jesus?'

'Is that a new American drink?' he replied. 'I only know Coke.'

The promoters of Coca-Cola have been more successful than the promoters of Jesus. Many children do not even know His name.

The Church could learn something from the merchants of this world, although it has an advantage that they do not have. It has not a product to sell, but a person to introduce; a person who has living water to give, so that one need never thirst again.

* * *

A boy of four had to play Joseph, and a girl of the same age Mary, in a Christmas play. The two children began to quarrel while they were on the stage.

The boy's father chided him. 'You forget what role you're playing! Joseph never quarrelled with Mary.'

The boy answered, 'How do you know?'

The father was dumbfounded. How *did* he know?

And in truth, he did not know.

However, we know from the Bible that the disciples quarrelled between themselves. Statues and pictures that show the saints always smiling are the inventions of grown-ups. Children know that saints on earth can be weak and earthly – especially if they live with parents who are Christians!

But if somebody happens to quarrel or commit some other sin, it does not mean that he ceases to be a saint. Christianity is not just a treasure and not just an earthen vessel. It is a treasure in an earthen vessel. Deny that the vessel exists, and you deny that the Christian exists.

* * *

When Mihai was five, he heard that the saints would one day walk with Jesus dressed in white garments. 'Does He have robes in children's sizes?' he enquired.

I assured him that they come in all sizes. St. Pancras and St. Tarcisius were devoured by wild beasts; they died as martyrs when they were only nine years old.

There are garments not only for those who are small and large in body, but also for those small and large in faith.

A bulldog, on seeing a pocket-sized poodle, demanded, 'Do you dare to call yourself a dog?'

The poodle replied, 'I admit that I am not as big as you are, but you certainly can't call me a cat. A small dog is still a dog!'

A feeble, fearful, backslidden Christian is still a Christian, and still has a white robe waiting for him.

* * *

A class of children was shown a painting of the Nativity, and told that the holy family was very poor.

'Then where,' queried a child, 'did they get the money to pay the photographer?'

The child's question could well prompt the reflection that it is good to share not only bread with the poor, but also the means of pleasure – such as provision for a family portrait!

* * *

A mother assured her child, who had confessed a sin, that 'the blood of Jesus has cleansed you from it.' The child thought for a moment, and then remarked, 'You said the same thing another time that I sinned. But where is Jesus' blood when we don't sin? What does it do then?'

In the words of a hymn:

> E'er since, by faith, I saw the stream
> Thy flowing wounds supply,
> Redeeming love has been my theme,
> And shall be till I die.

> (*William Cowper*, '*There is a fountain filled with blood*')

There is an unbroken stream of blood flowing from the wounds of Christ.

Blood flows constantly in our bodies, never pausing, never resting. It serves a hundred trillion cells, providing them with oxygen, amino acids, nitrogen and many other necessities. It carries away waste products and fights invaders. In the meantime, we go about our work without any awareness of what is happening inside us. Yet if the blood ceased to flow for a few brief moments, we would be dead.

In just the same way, the blood of the Saviour flows throughout His Church, nourishing it with heavenly manna, and bearing away sins.

Let His blood be an object of our devotion. We need it, even when we do not sin.

*   *   *

A child once asked her mother, 'If I had not been your little girl – what would I have been?' She could not imagine that she might not have existed at all. 'Non-existence', 'nirvana' – these are concepts that only adults wrestle with.

For years I was in solitary confinement, without books, without paper or pen, without ever hearing a voice or a whisper.

To occupy my time, I sometimes spent hours imagining what I would do in various situations. What would I do if I were pope – prime minister – a celebrated writer – pastor of a church – a millionaire – a beggar?

Once I tried to imagine that I was dead. I imagined myself in a coffin. Loved ones stood around weeping. A pastor said a prayer. Then I laughed heartily. 'If I can see myself in a coffin,' I thought, 'then I can't be dead!'

Many things are possible in life, and it is possible to imagine oneself in all sorts of situations. A soldier can dream of becoming emperor. It's possible – it happened to Napoleon. A beggar can become a millionaire. It's possible – I have known men who did. The reverse is also possible.

Because all these reversals of fate *are* possible, we can imagine them happening. But what is unimaginable is that we might cease to exist. Life is a gift of God, and it only finds fulfilment in eternal happiness.

The little girl found it impossible even to imagine never having existed.

* * *

Alex's curiosity is boundless. When he was five, he began to be suspicious about the origins of meat.

'Where do we get meat from?'

'From the supermarket.'

'But where does the supermarket get the meat from?'

'From cows.'

Alex's suspicions were confirmed. He became very grave. 'Do you mean that we kill cows so that we can eat their meat?'

'Yes.'

'Why?'

'Because we need nourishment.'

'But,' asked Alex, 'do we at least explain to the cows that that is why we kill them, and do we apologise to them for doing it?'

Very orthodox Jews do. I have seen their special 'slaughterers', whose religious function is to sing hymns while slaughtering animals. The kabbalistic purpose of doing so is to communicate somehow to unreasoning animals that they will be incorporated into the bodies of the chosen people, and will thereby become part of the temples of God, which is what our bodies are.

We ought to eat our meals with great devotion, remembering how many of God's creatures have been sacrificed so that we may live.

When Alex was six, and had heard the story of Cain and Abel for the umpteenth time, he said: 'In the beginning it was Cain who was good and Abel evil, because Abel killed a lamb, which is wrong, whereas Cain did not. Lambs are nice, living beings. Why did God order people to kill them for sacrifices?'

To kill a lamb wantonly – or, worse, to have somebody else kill one because I like eating lamb chops – is wrong. The Bible teaches that whatever we do we should do to the glory of God. Are we quite sure that He is glorified when we kill lambs?

Millions of animals are sacrificed each year just so that we can enjoy a good meal. But it is only justifiable to eat animals when it is done in the sole desire that our strengthened bodies may serve God better.

This is why the Talmud says, 'Every meal at which the subject of conversation is something other than the Word of God, is an idolatrous meal.'

(On the other hand, vegetarianism does not necessarily make men better. Cain did not kill a lamb, but he slew his brother; and Hitler was a strict vegetarian.)

*   *   *

A child was urged to eat carrots and peas because they contained vitamins, only to retort, 'Why didn't God put the vitamins in the sweets and ice-cream?'

My answer would have been, 'Because it's important for children not only to have vitamins, but also to learn to swallow what may be unpleasant to the taste.'

We all need to learn from the good and the unpleasant. A Christian must welcome unpleasant things sometimes, because they are part of the 'all things' that God is working together for our good.

*   *   *

Amelie at six listened to a sermon on Jesus' words, 'Let the little children come to me, and do not hinder them, for the kingdom of heaven belongs to such as these' (Matt. 19:14).

Turning to me she commented, 'But all men were once little children, and so they must have had the kingdom of heaven. How did they lose it?'

I remember my childhood sins very vividly. It does not require very much effort for most of us to remember how we lost our childhood innocence: lying, stealing, perhaps sliding downhill into a particular bad habit.

We had the kingdom, and we lost it. The Bible urges us

to return; we don't have to come to something entirely new, but simply to return to what was once ours, to the treasure that we lost.

* * *

A boy born in the satellite age was told by his father, 'We have just placed another star in the sky. We have launched a manned satellite.'

He asked, 'Who placed all the other stars in the sky?'

To this his father, who was not a believer, had no reply.

If it took so much genius and skill and intellectual brilliance to place into earth's orbit a satellite, manned by only a few people, a far greater intelligence must have been required to create the starry heavens.

The existence of man-made satellites is one more proof of the existence of God.

* * *

A child heard his father say 'Faith moves mountains', and asked him, 'Father, you believe in Christ. When did you last move a mountain?'

The father was embarrassed!

Jesus surely did not intend that we should move real mountains. One can imagine what chaos would be caused, were men to decide to move the Himalayas, the Rocky Mountains, the Carpathians or Alps according to whim!

But there are mountains of difficulty, of all kinds, that faith can move. Every believer should pay heed to this blessing of God. Then he will be able to say when he last moved a mountain!

* * *

When Amelie was eight, she asked me, 'You were once in a Communist jail. How did you come to the free world?'

I explained to her that Christian organisations had paid a ransom of £5,000 for my release.

'But,' she mused, 'you were in jail for fourteen years –

why did it take Western Christians so long to collect 10,000 dollars?'

I had no answer.

Others, who still suffer in Communist prisons, could have been helped long ago if it were not for our apathy. How much do we contribute towards easing their lot?

But the question goes even deeper.

When Hudson Taylor went as the first missionary to inland China, one of his first converts asked him, 'How long have you Englishmen known the gospel?'

'For 1,600 years,' he replied.

'Then why did you leave it so late to tell us about it? My parents and my ancestors died in sin, and went into the outer darkness.'

Why is it, that the good things in life seem to take so long to come to fruition?

I once discussed these matters with a child who, because he *was* a child, was not afraid to go even further in his thinking. 'God is like us,' he observed. 'He has promised that His kingdom would return. Jesus said, "Behold, I come quickly." But He tarries.'

Let us continue to pray, 'Thy kingdom come', and do all we can to hasten His coming. And let us 'never tire of doing what is right' (2 Thess. 3:13).

*   *   *

In Canada some children were asked to write down what they would ask the Pope if they were able to speak to him during his visit to their country.

They wrote down such questions as: 'What can I do to make God happier?', 'What can I do to help poor people?', 'How do you feel when you have to make decisions that will upset people?', and 'How do you feel about not being able to marry?'

Children ask direct questions; they are much less inclined to be devious than their elders. And they expect straight answers!

*   *   *

In front of Holman Hunt's well-known painting, 'Christ knocking at the door', a large group of visitors stood in admiration. One praised the colours; another noted the expression on Jesus' face; another called attention to the fact that the door had no outside knob, explaining that the heart can only be opened from the inside. Still another pointed out that the feet of Jesus were painted as turned away from the door; long accustomed to being rejected, He was prepared to depart.

Only one, a child, asked the question that really mattered: 'Father, did they let him in?'

It was a very small question. But it is the principal theme of the painting. All other aspects fade into insignificance.

* * *

A scientist was speaking to a group of children about Einstein's Theory of Relativity. A child raised the question: 'And what if Einstein was wrong?'

Only God can be totally trusted. All human assertions must be treated with a healthy scepticism.

A cardinal was once asked, 'What if scientists agreed unanimously that the statements of the Bible are untrue?'

The cardinal replied, 'I would wait a while! Scientists do not hold on to their certainties for very long.'

* * *

Once – I suppose it was from weariness – I protested to Amelie, then aged seven, 'You can't ask questions about everything!'

'Why not?'

'Because some things just happen. For example, Jesus said, "You hated Me without a cause." '

But still she persisted. 'Why isn't there a "Why" for everything?'

Even Einstein could not accept the theory of Heisenberg, the great German microphysicist, concerning the indeterminism of elementary particles. Heisenberg had shown that the law of causality, which was considered universal, has its limits; and therefore certain events have no 'why'.

Adults as well as children have to learn to simply accept certain facts that seem to do very well without our analysis and our categorisations as to cause and effect. It demands humility of mind. 'So much I know, and further, at this stage, I cannot go.'

The Hebrew Bible begins with the letter 'B' (*beth*), written ‎ב‎ – rather like a box with three walls. Hebrew text is read from right to left, so the opening in the 'box' faces forward. The rabbis explain that Scripture begins with this letter because it teaches that you will never know what is above, behind and below. And so we are to look forward, in the only direction in which God wishes to reveal Himself to us.

Amelie again: 'God must have known that Adam and Eve would sin. Why did He allow it?'

Again this 'Why' – the great 'Why'.

The response is simple. Sin is here, and we must fight it unceasingly. To waste time on fruitless 'Whys' is simply to sin all over again.

A person who has just been bitten by a rattlesnake will be foolish to waste time speculating about why he was attacked. Time is of the essence! The venom must be extracted – or he will die.

There are times when 'What' and 'How' are much more important than 'Why'.

*   *   *

Why so many questions, in a book about theology – even children's theology? Isn't theology a set of dogmatic statements?

No, it is not.

In the four Gospels, Jesus asks no less than 287 questions. His statements and assertions are far fewer in number.

His first recorded statement is a question: 'Why were

you searching for me?' (Luke 2:49). As a child in the temple, He, like children everywhere, spent His time simply listening and asking questions (cf. Luke 2:46).

As an adult He retained this childlike characteristic. Even on the cross, He asked a question: 'My God, my God, why have you forsaken me?' (Mark 15:34).

Later, confronting an enemy of His Church, He asked him a question: 'Saul, Saul, why do you persecute me?' (Acts 9:4).

When I first became a Christian and asked myself two vital questions, the only answers that I could find in the Bible were two further questions.

Firstly, I needed to know, which was the true Church? The Bible answered, 'Who is this that appears like the dawn, fair as the moon, bright as the sun, majestic as the stars in procession?' (S. of S. 6:10).

Secondly, I needed to know who was a reliable pastor to follow. Again the Bible replied with a question: 'Who then is the faithful and wise manager, whom the master puts in charge of his servants to give them their food allowance at the proper time?' (Luke 12:42).

The question is 'Who?': the reply is also, 'Who?'

Questions are an essential part of true theology. As Heidegger remarked, 'Questioning is the piety of thought.'

'For we know in part' (1 Cor. 13:9).

Answers

"I would like my father to walk out
of the frame and be with us again."

When Mihai was five, I came home one day and learned from my wife that he had committed some wrongdoing for which he needed to be punished. This time I decided to try a different approach. I left him alone.

The next morning, I told him the story of how Peter denied his Lord, and how, later, Jesus asked him three times: 'Do you love Me?' When I had told him the story, I asked Mihai, 'Do you love Jesus?'

'Yes,' said Mihai.

I asked him again, 'Do you love Jesus?' And again he answered, 'Yes.'

The third time I asked the question, he understood that I was chiding him for his sin of the day before. Tears came to his eyes as he said for the third time, 'Yes, I love Jesus.'

I thought that he might simply be repeating the words of Peter without really meaning them. So I asked him, 'How do you know that you really love Him?'

His thoughtful rejoinder was: 'Jesus did not ask Peter that. He was satisfied with the words, "I love you." '

Love really needs no explanation.

*   *   *

The comments of pre-school children indicate how much of positive value they can be taught, even at an early age.

Little Alex brightened our lives many times with his little pearls of wisdom.

'I like everybody in the whole world,' he said once, 'because I belong to God. All except the devil – because he put Jesus on the cross.'

Once, watching *Romeo and Juliet* on television, I tried to explain the plot to him. Later I asked him: 'Did you understand what was going on?'

His reply meant more than he knew. 'Yes – Grandma is Jesus' Juliet.'

He had understood, without theological ramifications, that Jesus' love for His own is like that of a bridegroom for his bride.

*   *   *

A child sat in his grandfather's arms as both of them looked in a mirror.

'Did God make us both?' he asked.

'Yes, of course.'

'Well, He does a much better job nowadays. He's had lots of practice! Now He doesn't put wrinkles on faces.'

God – improving?

Well, strange as it may seem to us, He says so about Himself: 'I will . . . do better unto you than at your beginnings' (Ezek. 36:11 AV).

The fact is, that God has given this generation more knowledge about health and much greater possibilities of learning than previous generations – at least, in the

Western world. May our young people respond by being more faithful to Him!

*   *   *

Linna was six years old. She asked a newly-married man, 'Do you love your bride?'

'Yes, of course,' was the quick rejoinder.

'That's good, because I imagine it must be awful to be married to a woman you don't love.'

The only basis for marriage is love between two people. Divorce is often the result when two people, pledged to love and care for each other, break their vows and abandon their commitments – unlike God, who keeps covenant with His bride, the Church, and is grieved when she is unfaithful (Matt. 23:37–38).

*   *   *

'Tell me something about Jesus, in whom you say you believe,' a man enquired of a young child.

The boy answered simply. 'I'm too small to say something great about Him.'

He did not know that he had repeated, almost verbatim, what Justin Martyr had said when asked to explain the mysteries of Christ. Justin was beheaded in the year AD 155.

*   *   *

'God is gigantic,' Alex pronounced, with childish finality.

I thought of John Mazzuconi, the Italian missionary who died a martyr's death in New Guinea at the beginning of the nineteenth century. Mazzuconi wrote, 'It is wrong to call the ocean immense. I traversed it in three months in a small ship. If one owned this whole world, he would own something smaller than a grain of sand. I wonder why so many fight to have it? Only One is truly immense, and He is eternal.'

*   *   *

Eusebius and John Chrysostom were both among those who praised the very young Christian child Barulas, who was brought before the heathen governor Asclepiades and asked: 'Which is better: to adore the one God who made heaven and earth, or a multitude of gods?'

The child replied, 'God is an almighty being. If there were many gods, they would become powerless, because the might of one would cancel out the might of another. God can be only one. Your gods are frauds.'

The tyrant demanded, 'Who has taught you these things?'

He replied, 'My mother, who was herself taught by God.'

The child was flogged and beheaded.

His mother herself carried him to the place of execution, and without shedding a tear, kissed him; and, telling him to remember her in heaven, gave him to the executioner.

* * *

We should not forget that it is to a child that we owe the writing of the most celebrated book about the holy Trinity.

Augustine was walking on the seashore meditating on this great mystery, about which he intended to write a book; but he could not develop his thoughts clearly. He was so frustrated that he was almost inclined to abandon the project.

Suddenly, he heard weeping. Running towards the sound, he found a child in tears. He asked what was the matter.

'Look what a big hole I have dug in the sand,' the child sobbed, 'but I cannot put the whole ocean in it. Can you?'

Augustine interpreted the question as a message sent to him by God Himself. Challenged by it, he wrote the book, but he wrote it with great modesty, realising that God is limitless and we are very small. Like the child on

the seashore, we can know only a very little about what –
and Who – lies beyond.

*   *   *

During a science lesson in school a pupil asked, 'Why did
God make the earth?'

Before the teacher had a chance to reply, a seven-year-
old boy gave the answer: 'So that people would have
something to stand on.'

He spoke a profound truth. This is why God gave
mankind the Law, the prophets, the Bible – even His own
Son.

*   *   *

A Pentecostal preacher patiently explained to Alex,
who was then five, the doctrines of his Church. He did
so with fervour, repeating again and again that this
was the only correct doctrine and that all others were
heresy.

I wanted to spare this preacher, by giving him the
impression that he was wasting his efforts on a child who
could not understand. So I asked Alex, 'Do you know
what the word "heresy" means?'

He replied straightforwardly. 'Sure I know! When you
have the right faith, you are happy. When heresy arrives,
your head begins to ache.'

The way of salvation is simple: 'Whoever believes and
is baptised will be saved.' Beware of things that cause
headaches!

*   *   *

Listening carefully to a narrative of the events that
led up to the crucifixion, Amelie at six concluded:
The disciples in Gethsemane were right when
they decided to flee. Peter was admonished for trying to
help. So why should the others have stayed? If they
were in the wrong, why did Jesus choose them in the first
place?'

Many a preacher has decried the weakness of the disciples in deserting Jesus on that dark night in Gethsemane. Curiously, the Gospels contain not one word of criticism or rebuke.

*　*　*

The distinguished psychologist Viktor Frankl was asked by his six-year-old daughter, 'Why do we speak of the "good" Lord?'

'Some weeks ago,' he reminded her, 'you had measles. The good Lord made you completely better.'

His daughter frowned. It was the wrong answer. 'But don't forget, Daddy, it was Him that sent me the measles in the first place!'

Children are not easily taken in by religious cant and cheap propaganda for God. They take His words seriously – 'Come now, let us reason together' (Isa. 1:18), which means that both sides have a say.

When children ask us why innocent people suffer, we have to confess to them that we simply do not have an explanation for this mystery. They do not respond to theological speculation about the whys and wherefores of pain.

Can a guinea pig in a laboratory understand its many sufferings? Is it aware that it serves the good of higher beings? Our sufferings may be of great value for the instruction of angels.

Let us not be afraid to admit how limited our human knowledge is. Children's questions lead to a theology that compels us to face up to our ignorance of many aspects of reality.

God is omniscient. We are not.

*　*　*

Six-year-old Alex had been throwing sand at other children, and as punishment had to report every day to the school principal. He asked his mother to write a letter of apology on his behalf, promising that it would never happen again. With this, the matter was settled. His father attempted to impress upon him the lesson to be learned from the episode. 'If you sin, you are hooked.' To which the reply came, 'But with promises, you can get off the hook!'

The prodigal son of Jesus' parable got away with even less. He promised nothing, but just uttered a few words that showed his repentance. It was enough. He had a loving father.

*   *   *

Somebody asked a child what one must do before receiving forgiveness of sin. The candid reply was, 'Sin!' There could not have been a better answer.

That is why the Catholic Church sings '*O felix culpa*' – 'O blessed sin, which gave us such a Saviour'.

*   *   *

E. Stanley Jones, the renowned missionary to India, told a story about a child whose teacher asked him, 'What would you like for Christmas?'

Looking up at a picture of his father, who was dead, the child said wistfully, 'I would like my father to walk out of the frame and be with us again.'

Children love their parents by instinct. When you stop loving your parents, you have stopped being what Jesus wants you to be – childlike.

*   *   *

One child asked another: 'What does it mean, to be a real man? Does it hurt?'

The other child replied, 'It hurts a great deal. Grandma is a real woman, and look how many wrinkles she has! But only unreal people think that is ugly. I love her!'

*   *   *

A teacher once asked her class, 'What does the Bible contain?'

A girl replied: 'In our Bible there are a lot of dates, marriages, deaths, newspaper clippings, a birthday card, a Christmas card, and that's about all.'

Children who are brought up in homes where that is all they can find in the Bible are in great spiritual danger.

What is in your Bible?

*   *   *

A five-year-old boy had recited his usual bedtime prayer: 'Now I lay me down to sleep, I pray the Lord my soul to keep; If I should die—'

Here he stopped, and asked, 'Daddy, what's dying like?'

'It's dark,' replied the father, for that was all he knew. The little questioner remained awake in the dark, sobbing uncontrollably.

Another child had a father who sent him to Sunday school. He knew that his mother had a terrible fear of dying. One Sunday he came home from church in great excitement.

'Mother! You don't have to be afraid of dying any more, because Jesus went through the tomb and left a light behind Him!'

Jesus submitted to the power of death, and was entombed. But He had the power of resurrection, and He promises us this same experience if we commit our lives to Him.

'Death' is the name given to a deep sleep, by those who do not know about resurrection. But Jesus has the keys to the grave. He knows how to give life to those who die. The proof lies in His empty tomb.

*   *   *

A child who had just said his morning prayers was asked by his mother, 'What did you pray about?'

'I told Him to rest,' he said. 'I told Him to sleep in peace, because I'm awake now.'

Love calls for reciprocity. Jesus says, 'Come unto Me,

and I will give you rest.' May we not say the same thing to Him, with all our hearts?

*   *   *

A Christian girl was once asked by a friend, 'How do you begin to love Jesus? I don't love Him – I can't see any reason why I should. I can't make myself love Him.'

The girl replied, 'Don't try! Just repeat to yourself, "Jesus loves me," over and over again. It was through Him that the flowers, the birds, and everything beautiful were created; He went through a lifetime of suffering, and died on the cross in great sorrow, for me; He has prepared for me a heaven of exquisite beauty; He offers me forgiveness for all my sins and a life full of joy. He loves me, for sure! Never try to love Him. Just say again and again, "He loves me."'

Later the other girl confided, 'I love Him.'

What a model of Christian witness! And what a sermon in miniature!

*   *   *

A father once noticed that his son was reading the Bible a great deal, and he asked him why. 'I'm preparing for my final exam,' he said.

His motive was a good one.

*   *   *

Little Alex was asked, 'How would you make a painting of love?'

'Two people kissing,' he answered.

'How would you paint death?'

'A man lying in a coffin, with a red cross on it. The cross saves.'

'And how would you paint life?'

'I'd paint a man and the sun.'

It is not just the things that children say that are remarkable, but also their drawings. Those reproduced below were drawn by a four-year-old girl whose father was convicted of raping her repeatedly.

MY MOM

MY DAD

In her drawings the middle part of both bodies is omitted. It was abhorrent to her to think about that part of the body. The father has no legs; they are replaced by phallic symbols. She has scrawled over his face, reflecting the anger she feels towards him.

If a child knew me as I really am, how would he or she draw me?

*   *   *

J. Allen Blair told of a proud Sunday school teacher, who was attempting to explain to children how they should practise the virtue of obedience.

As he strode up and down the platform, everything about his outward appearance betrayed his self-esteem – his head was held high, his chest was thrust out, his gestures were commanding.

'Now, children,' he boomed, pausing to fix them with a stare, 'why do people call me a Christian?' He was clearly expecting somebody to respond with 'Because you are obedient to Christ.'

But a boy raised his hand and ventured, 'People call you a Christian because they don't know you well enough.'

Little children find it hard to disguise their true feelings, especially when they are talking about other people. Telling falsehoods is something that they learn later, often out of fear of punishment (though sometimes what is thought to be lying is in fact the child's imagination).

Adults tend to be much less candid in what they say to each other's face. Instead they learn the virtue of 'tact', which is shown up as hypocrisy when they gossip about an individual behind his or her back.

It is sometimes necessary to meet evil head-on, with a child's directness. John the apostle, who wrote so extensively and so beautifully about love, nevertheless had this to say about Diotrephes ('who loves to be first'): 'I will call attention to what he is doing, gossiping maliciously about us' (3 John 10).

In the words of a wise man, '[There is] a time to be silent and a time to speak' (Eccles. 3:7). Children's theology 'tells it like it is'!

* * *

Children know how to apply what they have learned, but sometimes they do it in unexpected ways.

A boy complained to his mother that his stomach ached, and she said, 'It's probably because your stomach is empty. I'll make you a snack.'

Not long afterwards, a pastor visited the house. He mentioned that he had a headache, upon which the child observed: 'Probably, Pastor, it's because your head is empty. You should feed it with something.'

* * *

When pupils in a school in England were asked to name the person with whom they would most like to be stuck in a lift, a girl answered, 'A lift specialist!'

In a very real sense, we are all 'stuck' – not in a lift, but on a planet bent on self-destruction. We go through life like a train that roars through the darkness towards an unknown destination. The problems of our own lives are already too complicated for us, but when they are multiplied by the threats of nuclear war, the population explosion, pollution, increasing immorality, crime and violence, they are too much to bear. Perplexed and afraid, we can see no way out.

Jesus is a specialist in human tragedy. His was the most tragic of all human lives. Poor, oppressed, rejected, scorned, spat upon, whipped, crucified, buried – He offered the only solution to the world's problems: the power of His resurrection.

Let us prefer the Specialist to anybody else!

* * *

An atheist once said, in reply to a child who had claimed to be a Christian, 'I will give you a pound if you can show me where your God is!'

The child replied, 'I only have a fifty-pence piece, but I will give it to you if you can show me a place where God is not.'

* * *

Addressing a group of schoolboys, a bishop gave the following example of 'moral courage': 'A boy in a dormitory, who, in front of everybody, kneels and says his prayers before hopping into bed.'

He asked the boys if they could think of another example.

'Sir,' a voice piped up, 'a bishop in a dormitory full of bishops, who hops into bed *without* saying his prayers.'

Bishops and prelates rarely have that courage! But biblical authors like David, Job and Jeremiah had the courage to complain to God, using words that to us might seem blasphemous. We ourselves would probably have suppressed such thoughts, and the result would have been that they would have become submerged and unresolved within us.

Children teach us to have the courage not only to tell God that we love Him, but also to argue with Him. In the words of a hymn, He has 'the answer to all our questionings'. By the same token, He will surely accept us when the questions are hard ones.

Prayers

Nadia reached up and
handed him the
flowers.

I was once a guest in a Christian home. I was rather depressed, brooding about all the things that I do not possess.

The children's bedtime arrived. A boy who was not four years old prayed. 'I thank You, God, for my hair, my face, my eyebrows, my eyelids, both my eyes, my cheeks, my nose, my lips, my teeth, my tongue . . .' On and on he continued, until he had itemised everything down to the soles of his feet. He finished his prayer with the request 'Make my Daddy and our guest happy.'

His prayer was answered, as I realised that I possessed

all the same things that the child did – and mine came in a bigger size! I was also aware of other aspects of my being, about which he had not yet learned. But I had never recited them all in a prayer of thankfulness.

'A little child shall lead them' – even in prayer.

* * *

In Sunday school a pastor showed the children a telephone. He explained, 'You speak on the telephone to people whom you cannot see. It's the same with prayer. You call God, and He listens. Don't be distressed that you can't see Him. We speak to people we cannot see, every day.'

A boy asked, 'Pastor, what is God's telephone number?'

The pastor could have replied something like this: 'It is a five-figure number: repentance, faith in Jesus' sacrifice, love, truth and righteousness.'

* * *

During a prayer meeting a restless child continued to misbehave after several warnings. Finally his exasperated mother said to him, 'Come outside with me. You're going to get a spanking!'

As he left the boy called out to the group, 'Pray for me! Mother hits hard!'

Impressed by his plea, his mother decided not to spank him. When they came back, he greeted the believers with: 'You see? Prayer works!'

* * *

A girl who had been naughty was sent to bed and advised to pray to God that He would take away her bad temper.

She knelt and prayed: 'Dear God, please take away my bad temper. And Mother's.'

We always need to pray from both sides of a situation.

* * *

A child prayed, 'Dear God, please convince Father that
he should not spank me any more. You will remember
that I have already asked You to do this. How many times
do I have to tell You the same thing?'

We can take risks in prayer.

* * *

I overheard a girl praying 'Dear God, be nice and obey
your mother.' I remembered that there was a time when
God was on earth in the person of Jesus Christ.

It cannot have been easy either for the virgin Mary or
for Joseph to have such a child. I wonder, did His
uniqueness ever seem to them to be merely self-will? The
fact that there was some distance between the child and
His parents can be inferred from His words to His mother
when He was twelve years old, and she had sought Him
for three days: 'Why were you searching for Me?' (Luke
2:49).

He was obedient, in His own way. But when His
mother asked a special favour from Him at the wedding
in Cana, He answered, 'Dear woman, why do you in-
volve Me?' Perhaps when He was small, Joseph might
occasionally have said to Him, 'Please obey your
mother.'

* * *

In a morning prayer, little Dorothy said, 'Thank you,
God, for this beautiful morning. My dog will enjoy it.'

She had a breadth of vision. The Bible's vision is even
broader. God feeds the birds of the air and the beasts of
the field, so satisfying their needs. He also makes the sun
shine and the rain fall on the evil as well as the good.

Let us, like this little child, appreciate the joys given to
others, whether or not we share in them.

* * *

I once stayed in the home of a farmer, whose three-year-old Carlitos always prayed for 'Daddy, Mommy, Grandma, the sheep, the goats, the guinea-hen, the dogs, and the cat.'

Do we pray like that, in detail – or in mere generalities, like 'God bless the missionaries'?

Jesus prayed for Peter by name.

*   *   *

When he was only five, Alex prayed, 'Dear God, take good care of Father, Mother – and also of Yourself. If anything happens to You, we'll all be in trouble.'

It was not a unique prayer. Peter the disciple prayed that Jesus would not go to His death. He was afraid that their entire group would be in trouble without Him.

We can all pray not only *to* God, but also *for* God – that His name might be hallowed, His kingdom come, and His will be done.

*   *   *

A father and his little son sat down at the counter of a small cafeteria for a bite to eat. 'We'll have a silent prayer,' said the adult, and bowed his head.

Minutes passed. The boy's eyes remained closed. When he finally looked up, his father asked him, 'What were you praying about for so long?'

'How could I know how long my prayer was?' asked the son. 'You told me it was to be a silent prayer!'

He may well have known more about silent prayer than his father did. A silent prayer is one in which not only the lips, but also the mind keeps silent. In mental prayer one should close the mind's door and let no distracting thoughts enter – not even the thought of time passing.

The first disciples met behind locked doors out of fear of the Jews, who could only destroy their bodies. So how much more carefully should we lock the door when we pray silently, so that no thievish idea may enter which might destroy the soul. The Lord can enter through locked doors; and we desire no other guest.

Mental prayer means a time that is spent in the embrace of Jesus, our heavenly Bridegroom. And what bride, in such an ecstasy, could tell you how long it has lasted?

* * *

During the night a loud knocking sounded at the door of the Danielsky family in Russia.

'Open up! It's the police!'

The mother whispered quickly, 'What should I do with the Bible? They'll take it away.'

'Open the door quickly – or we'll break it down!'

Piotr, the little boy, had a sudden idea. He took the Bible and placed it under the blanket on his sister's doll's bed. To Nadia, who was even smaller than he was, he whispered, 'Don't pay any attention to the people who are coming in. Just carry on playing with the doll, in her bed.' Quietly, he prayed, 'Lord, please keep the Bible safe for us.'

It was many hours later that the police left, taking with them their plunder of hymnals and other books. When they had gone, Nadia retrieved the Bible from the doll's bed. 'The credit belongs to Piotr,' she said.

Piotr replied, 'Let us thank God. I prayed that they would not find the Bible, and He heard my prayer.'

May we all cherish the Bible as tenderly as Piotr did!

* * *

Because of his faith in Christ, Nadia's father was in a Soviet jail. She was walking one day with her grieving mother through a meadow.

Turning to her, Nadia said thoughtfully, 'Be at peace, Mummy. God, who takes care of these flowers, will also care for Daddy.' She picked a few flowers and prayed: 'Dear God, please make it possible for Daddy to have these flowers.'

The next day she accompanied her mother to the police station to leave a parcel of food for the prisoner. Nadia smiled at the officer on duty. 'Do you have any children?' she asked.

He looked down at her. She was very like the young daughter he had recently buried.

Nadia reached up and handed him the flowers that she had picked, saying, 'Uncle, please give these to my Daddy. You will, surely, won't you?'

The torturer was no match for the little girl. The prisoner received the flowers.

God does indeed answer prayer.

* * *

It was Nadia's birthday. 'Lord Jesus,' she prayed, 'last year on this day my father brought me a bar of chocolate' – chocolate is a luxury in Russia – 'but now, he is in jail. You are my only hope. Please bring me some chocolate.'

Larissa, her older sister, rebuked her. 'We are only allowed to pray for absolute necessities, not for dainties.'

Her mother agreed. 'We can only ask for food when we are hungry, or for clothes when our old ones are worn out. We can also pray for health if we are ill. But I don't think that chocolate is a necessity of life.'

There was a knock at the door. It was their pastor. He had known nothing of the birthday, but something had made him buy chocolate for the children.

It was a lesson for Nadia's family, and for the rest of us. Our God is a bountiful God! Sometimes He takes delight in answering prayers for things which are not absolute necessities.

* * *

Once, when Mihai was small, we left him with a baby-sitter. Before going to bed, he prayed with her. He asked God to bring us back home immediately.

After the prayer, he said to the babysitter, 'Please open the door. My parents will be waiting there.'

We actually were! I had discovered that I had forgotten to take any money with me.

Mihai was triumphant. 'I *knew* my prayer would be answered!'

May we have such childlike faith.

* * *

When he was a boy, Robert Louis Stevenson remarked to his mother, 'Mama, one cannot be good without praying.'

'How do you know, Robert?'

'Because,' he said with an air of great finality, 'I've tried.'

It might be valuable, I suggest, to try a childish experiment. Decide to spend one whole day without prayer. Then, in the evening, examine yourself and see whether you have succeeded in being good without it (Be honest!).

* * *

A little fellow was sent to bed early because he had been naughty. Soon he reappeared. 'I've been thinking about what I did,' he told his mother. 'And I said a prayer.'

'That's fine – if you asked your heavenly Father to make you good.'

'Oh no, I said something else; I asked Him to make my mother put up with me as I am.'

In the Greek New Testament, *aphiemi* means 'to forgive' and 'to leave'. In the Lord's prayer, the text can be read either as 'Forgive us our trespasses,' or 'Leave us our trespasses.'

Each of us is a cluster of selves. One part of me wants to be forgiven, while another part is very much attached to a given sin and wants to be allowed to keep it.

One voice in us asks the Father to make us into saints; another says, 'Put up with me, just as I am.'

As adults, we repress this second voice. A child, lacking our inhibitions, openly expresses this other side of his being. It is better to expose and then expunge our self-centred attitudes than to repress them and deny that they exist.

The Psalmist said, 'I . . . did not cover up my iniquity . . . and you forgave the guilt of my sin' (Ps. 32:5).

* * *

When she was asked whether she prayed every day, a little girl replied, 'Not quite every day – some days, I don't need anything.'

She was right not to make prayer just a routine. But if we have nothing to ask God for, then let us thank Him for that! And let us praise Him continually.

* * *

At a family gathering, little Alex prayed aloud as we knelt together. 'God is great; God is good; and I thank Him for the food.'

My wife gently chided him. 'Why did you pray like that? It's not time for a meal.'

'That's not my fault,' Alex responded stoutly. 'I've said grace, now it's up to you to give me something to eat!'

He had touched on a profound truth. It is written in Scripture, 'Faith is being sure of what we hope for and certain of what we do not see' (Hebrews 11:1). Let us thank God for His blessings whether or not we have yet received them. Then it is His responsibility to ensure that we receive them – and He will not fail.

Jesus said, 'Have faith in God . . . If anyone . . . does not doubt in his heart but believes that what he says will happen, it will be done for him' (Mark 11:22–23).

* * *

The well-known Christian psychiatrist, Paul Tournier, tells how as a small boy he used to dream of doing some great deed.

With a toy construction set, he began to build a strange machine, bristling with springs and gears. One day, he confided his ambition to his young sister. The machine was to be capable of creating life.

She asked him to explain how it would work, but Paul was vague about that. He admitted that he would have to rely on prayer. He would pray hard, and God would work through the machine.

'If that is so,' exclaimed his sister, 'what are all the gears for?'

What are our many gears for?

Once we have prayed, we must be patient. Even if it seems impossible, we must quietly put up with our impatience and allow God to work. He hears us, and he answers us.

* * *

Billy Graham has five children. One day at family prayers he was jolted by his son Franklin, who interrupted his father's exposition of Scripture with the words, 'Daddy, let's not talk so much – let's pray more.'

Even a child understood that talking to God is more valuable than mere human talk.

But how we love our own talk!

* * *

A friend of ours died in circumstances that caused his family to doubt his salvation.

Amelie, who was then seven, comforted them with these words: 'I'm positive that he is in heaven. He was very nice to me. I prayed for him. I said to Jesus, "God promised Rahab, who did a favour for some Jews who were in trouble, that she and all her house would be saved [cf. Josh. 2]. This man belongs to my household. He is in my heart." There is no doubt that he is saved!'

When Jesus saw the faith of the men who brought the paralytic to Him (not the faith of the paralytic himself) then, we are told, He honoured them with a miracle of healing on their friends' behalf.

* * *

Allenby was the British general who freed Jerusalem

from Turkish rule during World War I, without firing a single shot.

When he was a boy he used to repeat his evening prayers after his mother. They always ended with these words: 'Dear Lord, we would not forget Thine ancient people Israel. Hasten the day when Israel will again be Thy people and will be restored to Thy favour and their land.'

What joy it must have given the God of Israel, to hear an English boy pray such a prayer! In His good providence, God allowed Allenby to become the man to fulfil his childhood prayers.

*   *   *

Dwight L. Moody, the noted evangelist, used to go into saloons with a little boy named Tommy, who really knew how to pray. If Moody's exhortations met with a cool reception, Tommy would perch on a barrel of wine and begin praying aloud. He then kept on praying until he had 'prayed out' all the drunkards. Many were converted through his simple, yet effective, ministry.

*   *   *

A little girl prayed, 'Dear Lord, please make all the bad people good and all the good people nice.'

We can learn from children how to wrap goodness in cheerfulness.

*   *   *

When a Rumanian child heard, for the first time, that a book exists in which are contained the names of all who will enter Paradise, he knelt and prayed: 'God, please write me down. My name is Rada Ionescu. I'd better spell it for you, so that there will be no mistake.' And he carefully pronounced each letter.

Then he added, 'Other people may have the same name as me. So, please note my name and address, and my date of birth, to avoid any confusion.'

Are we as precise and careful in our own relationships with God?

*   *   *

An eight-year-old boy in America prayed, 'Father, my Daddy sometimes lets me sit on his lap and steer the car – but he puts both hands over mine. Please, put Your hands over those of the President as he rules our country, to keep it safe.'

The prayers of young children are often full of insight.

*   *   *

A child knew he had done something very wrong. He had told his mother a lie. So he prayed, 'O God, make it not to have happened.'

This is not such an unreasonable prayer as it might seem. God can undo events for us. We regret having committed a sinful deed. We know it was as red as scarlet. Remorse cannot undo something done. Repentance obtains forgiveness, but how can the lie, murder, adultery, blasphemy or whatever it might be, be erased from history?

God can do even this. He makes sins that are scarlet as white as snow (Isaiah 1:18).

When Jesus changed water into wine at Cana, it was into the best wine, which is old wine. The liquid He gave to the wedding guests was not something which had formerly been water and had suddenly become wine. His miracle was profounder than that. In place of the water was something that had always been wine.

For King Hezekiah, God caused the sundial to go back ten degrees (Isaiah 38:8). Suppose this happened at 6 p.m. Miraculously, it was again 8 a.m. on the same day. He had said rash words to his wife, he might have been harsh with a servant, he might have issued a bad decree – but it was as if things had never happened.

God gave back to Hezekiah the day that had passed. In the spiritual realm this is possible. The same can be true of us in our daily lives. The child was right in praying 'God, make my lie not to have happened.'

Interpretations

"Look, your heads are bent!
You must straighten up too."

A Christian child, aged ten, had been brought up on the
Bible and its teachings about love. But there was a great
deal of quarrelling in his family.

One day, following a harsh exchange of words
between his parents, he approached his father. 'Daddy,'
he said, 'please take me to an oculist, and to an ear
specialist.'

'Why, son?'

'Well, there must be something wrong with me. I can't

see the things I hear in the Bible, and I can't hear the things I see.'

Many of us would have to say the same. Jesus is the Word who became flesh. Our faith must be seen also in the flesh.

*　　*　　*

'Alex, get in the car,' urged his mother. 'I'm taking you to the doctor.'

'Why?' asked the five-year-old.

'Because of the cough.'

They came from the doctor's surgery to my house. Alex was happy and carefree. 'The doctor hasn't got a cough,' he told me. 'We went to see him, and he's OK!'

Hearing him say this, I told him once again the story of my conversion. Somebody who loved my soul brought me to Jesus, though I felt no need of Him. The friend told me that I must come to Him because of my sin. But I emerged happy from that first meeting with Jesus. I had discovered that *He* has no sin. He is clean and pure. This gave me a joy that has lasted for half a century.

If Jesus had committed a single sin, He could never have helped a single sinner. But because He was without any sin, the sinner can have confidence that all his transgressions are forgiven.

The last word is with Alex: 'So it's the same with Jesus as with my doctor! If you are taken to him with a cough, you are glad that he hasn't got a cough himself.'

*　　*　　*

When he was six, Alex sat looking at a picture of Golgotha. 'They killed the one who was good, and they killed those who were bad. But this is wrong. They ought not to have killed the robbers like that. Jesus? Yes. They were right to crucify Him, because His death opened up the gates of heaven for us. But robbers should only be locked up.'

Do we judge and speak evil of good and bad men?

*   *   *

A little French girl named Bernadette told her priest and her whole village that the virgin Mary had repeatedly appeared to her. This happened in Lourdes, and since then the village has become a world-famous place of pilgrimage.

Catholics believe in the objective reality of Bernadette's vision; Protestants would prefer to say that she had a subjective experience, because she was used to venerating Mary. These differing opinions, however, do not alter the value of the following episode.

An unbeliever asked Bernadette, 'What kind of expression did the Virgin have? Was she frowning? Was she sad? Did she smile?'

Bernadette replied, 'She was smiling.'

'Then show me how she smiled.'

Bernadette, so the story goes, smiled with an inimitable expression of mingled compassion, tolerance, grief for sin, painful surprise, and hopeful expectation.

The unbeliever fell to his knees. 'Now I believe!'

I have myself witnessed a similar incident in jail.

Have you ever looked attentively at the smile of a child who has a personal relationship with the Saviour? In that smile, all heaven is mirrored.

*   *   *

A girl of ten learned that the gospel must be preached to every creature, and she came to the conclusion that this must also apply to stalks of wheat. Were they not created by God?

But what should she preach to them?

She went into the field, and shouted, 'The Bible commands us to make His paths straight. Look, your heads are bent! You must straighten up, too!'

We should call upon everyone to 'straighten up'. And

the stalks of wheat? They bow as a mark of gratitude to the earth, for nurturing them with water and minerals.

*   *   *

My wife and I are Jewish Christians. When Mihai was five, we took him to the synagogue on *Simhat Torah* (literally, 'the rejoicing in the Law'), which is the festival commemorating the giving of the Law on Sinai. The scroll of the Law is taken around the synagogue, and the people, especially the children, press forward to kiss it.

When the procession came near us, Mihai asked me, 'Should I kiss the scroll?'

'It's up to you,' I said. I had previously explained to him the significance of the day and the ceremony.

The rabbi approached, and lowered the scroll so that Mihai could kiss it.

'Thank you,' said the child, 'but I will not kiss it.'

The procession came to a halt, and hundreds of pairs of eyes focused on him in consternation. Mihai, by now extremely tense, repeated his words: 'I will not kiss it.'

When the service was over, the president of the synagogue, who was a friend of mine, asked Mihai, 'Why did you do that?'

'Sir,' he said, 'God has given us mothers for kissing. The Law of God was given to be read and obeyed, not to be kissed.'

In Orthodox Churches also, the Gospel, luxuriously bound, is paraded so that all the communicants can kiss it. Few ever read it, and fewer attempt to obey it.

*   *   *

There is a Jewish legend that Terah, Abraham's father, was a manufacturer of idols. He made small wooden figures of the gods and sent his son to the market place to sell them.

But as soon as the boy Abraham found a buyer, he would say to him, 'I can see that you are an elderly person. Perhaps you are sixty or seventy years old.

So how can this god which my father made yesterday possibly help you?'

So he returned home at the end of the day with his merchandise unsold, and his father would beat him.

One day, he decided to test the reality of these gods for himself. In Terah's home was a chapel containing a series of wooden gods, with the figure of the chief god in the centre. Little Abraham asked his mother to prepare a fine stew, which he planned to offer as a sacrifice to these so-called 'heavenly powers'.

He presented the food to the chief god, and knelt before it to see what would happen. The hours went by and still the god made no move. Finally Abraham took an axe and smashed all the gods except the chief one, into whose arms he placed the axe.

His father returned and found the idols hacked to pieces. He asked what had happened, and the boy replied, 'I presented some food to them. They quarrelled over who should have it, and the big fellow killed the smaller ones.'

'Don't be stupid,' said his father. 'They can't see, or speak, or move.'

'Then they are no gods,' replied Abraham, and with a rapid movement he destroyed the last idol.

Then he wandered far from his father's house, wondering all the time who had made the world.

He saw the moon rising, and said to himself, 'This must be he!'; and he adored it. But after a few hours, the moon set and the sun rose. 'Aha, this must be he!' he cried, and so he adored the sun.

But the sun also set. Then he thought, 'There must be someone who alternates the sun and the moon.'

He passed by a house and noticed a number of white linen cloths in the garden. Later, returning by the same road, he saw that the cloths were no longer white but many-coloured. There was no one to be seen, but he deduced: 'There must be a man in the house. He is probably a dyer, and he has coloured the cloths. Likewise, in the heavens I can see no one, but I can see the colour of the sky change every day. There must be an invisible Master!'

And Abraham became a worshipper of the invisible God.

*   *   *

When Amelie was nine, she came to me one day with a serious question: 'Grandpa, are we allowed to say something when we know that God is wrong, or do we have to swallow our questions and keep quiet?'

I replied, 'Great men of God, like David and Job, spoke frankly with God when they sometimes had the impression that He was in the wrong. You can do that too. But what is it that has made you dissatisfied?'

'Two things. Firstly, He ought not to have given commandments. Daddy gives commandments as well. One should only give advice. Secondly, surely God was wrong when He said "Love your neighbour as yourself." We don't love ourselves very well. We torment ourselves and make our lives unhappy. If we were to love our neighbours like that, it would be awful for them! We have to love them *better*.'

As regards Amelie's first criticism of God, she is correct; but the fault lies not with Him but with the translators of the Bible. What we call 'Commandments' are not commandments at all, but expressions of desires and enablings. The Hebrew language does not use the imperative, but the so-called 'jussive' tense. The prohibitions do not begin with the imperative (which in the Hebrew is *lo*), but with *al*, which conveys a desire.

A correct translation would be, 'Please do not kill,' 'Please do not steal,' and so on. Or, more to the point, 'If you love Me, you will not kill,' and so on.

As regards Amelie's second criticism, she is right again. To love your neighbour only as well as you love yourself would be inadequate. Jesus taught a better way:

'As I have loved you, so you must love one another' (John 13:34). There is no greater love than to give your life for another.

*　　*　　*

After a sermon on obedience, a mother sought to reinforce the message for her child: 'You heard what the pastor said – you must obey your parents.'

The child replied, 'You seem to have missed the other part of the sermon. Are you obedient to father?'

We all have filters; we often hear in sermons only what suits our interests and inclinations.

*　　*　　*

A little boy in New York wrote the following letter to God.

Dear God, if You do all these things, You are pretty busy. Now, here is my question: What is the best time for me to talk to You? I know You are always listening – but when do You listen to New York?

Perhaps it had occurred to the child that God does not listen to every place at every time. For certain places, it can be too late for God to listen. It is now too late for Sodom and Gomorrah for Capernaum and Bethsaida, just as there was a 'too late' for Esau after he had lost the blessing.

It is better to make arrangements ahead of time. God longs for human beings to communicate with Him. He is so anxious for us to do so that He says, 'Before they call, I will answer' (Isa. 65:24).

*　　*　　*

A group of children were watching the space shuttle *Discovery* taking off like a ball of fire.

A little boy shouted, 'God is putting a new star in the sky!'

You can smile and say, 'This is a star that will last only a few days.' But all stars have only a finite existence. They appear, grow and die, like everything else in our knowable universe.

But there is a God who has put them into the sky. He also sends aloft the *Discovery*, according to laws that He has ordained, and through the medium of human hands and minds which are also His creation.

Children grasp this and go straight to the First Cause, just as the Bible does:

'In the beginning, God' (Gen. 1:1).

*　　*　　*

Amelie was asked a riddle. A man on a river bank has a wolf, a lamb, and a cabbage. He wants to get them safely on to the other bank, and the condition is that he can take only one at a time in his boat. How is he to do it? If he takes the wolf first, the sheep will eat the cabbage. If he takes the cabbage first, the wolf will eat the sheep. He can take the sheep first, but on the next crossing he will have to take either the cabbage or the wolf; in both cases, one of the objects will be eaten on the opposite shore.

Some of the adults who were present hazarded a few guesses. Finally Amelie said, 'We should hasten the Lord's return through prayer and preaching, for when that happens the lion and the sheep will be friends. The cabbage will be safe, too, because the kingdom of God is not a matter of food and drink' (cf. Rom. 14:17).

For her, the Lord's return was a certainty, upon which she counted to solve the problems of life. Sadly, it rarely enters into the calculations of adults. That is why He will return for the children of God; for children He counts, He is important.[1]

*　　*　　*

---

1. If you want to find the original solution of the riddle, remember that what is taken to the far bank by boat can also be brought back!

A four-year-old toddler had his own version of the pledge to the American flag:

> I pledge allegiance to the flag of the United States, and to the Republic for which it stands; one nation under God, indivisible, with liberty and Jesus [instead of 'justice'] for all.

* * *

One morning, a boy said to his father, 'I dreamed about God last night.'

'What was He doing in your dream?'

'He was locked in a cupboard. He was begging me to let Him out. What does it mean, Daddy?'

The father could have answered that when we shut Jesus out of our lives, it is as if we were locking Him in a cupboard, and all His powers of love and goodness with Him. Let us unlock the door, and let Him enter our lives.

The Bible uses a slightly different image: Jesus says, in effect, 'Behold, I stand at the door of your heart and knock. If you let Me in [He never enters uninvited], I will come in and eat with you, and share My bounties with you' (cf. Rev. 3:20).

* * *

In Russia some children were taken from parents who had taught them about God. In the atheistic boarding school to which they were sent, they were given a doll.

When they thought they were unobserved, the children decided to play at 'prayer meetings'. But they found that the doll's knees did not bend and so it could not kneel.

One of the children went to the teacher. 'Please can I have another doll? This one is plain stupid.'

'Why do you say that?'

'Well, everyone who does not kneel before God must be stupid.'

It was a witness to the Communist teacher.

* * *

A sixteen-year-old Arab father took his baby girl to an Arab orphanage in Israel. Her fourteen-year-old mother had died in childbirth. If the child had been a boy, the father's family would have looked after it, but they had no use for a girl.

The young father visited the child, Muna, regularly. As she grew older she looked forward joyfully to his visits, and would wait for him to arrive, crying 'Baba [Daddy] comes!'

Every time he came she clung to him, begging him not to leave, or at least to take her with him.

Eventually he remarried and decided not to visit any more. His new wife did not want the child, and he could not bear his daughter's weeping.

Muna was devastated. She refused to eat or drink, and sat at the door, repeating over and over again, 'Baba comes.' No one could make her give up her self-imposed fast. Finally she had to be force-fed.

Still she continued to insist, 'Baba comes!' A missionary tried to tell her about a heavenly father, but she would not listen. One Baba had abandoned her. Why have another, who would probably be no better?

Fortunately the missionary was able to convince her that the heavenly Father is an entirely different kind of Baba, a Baba whose love never fails. Muna became once more a happy child.

Too many of us accept the notion of a heavenly Father who might forsake us or let us down. Who needs a Father like that? Have we not been forsaken by enough humans? Why open ourselves up to another bitter experience?

But this picture of the heavenly Father is a false one. He loves to the uttermost. He runs to meet the returning prodigal. He gives him the finest robe. He kills the fatted calf in his honour. Then He says, 'What more can I do, to prove I love you?' (cf. Isa. 5:1–4).

*   *   *

When Mihai was four or five, he asked me, 'How was Jesus born?'

He had heard the story many times, but I told him again how Jesus was born in a stable, how the shepherds and magi visited Him, and so on.

'I know all that,' he said. 'But I'm curious about something else. I've often heard you quote the proverb, "Whatever is born of a cat, eats mice." But if Jesus had been born like us, He would have been bad like us. So He must have been born entirely different.'

Intuition like that has enabled Christians through the centuries to believe in the revelation of the virgin birth of Jesus.

*   *   *

The 'Christian Mission to the Communist World', having received news of a Lithuanian Christian who had been imprisoned for his faith, sent a parcel to his mother.

To their great surprise, they received a letter of thanks from the prisoner himself; because of a serious injury, he had been released before completing his sentence.

He wrote:

Working as a slave-labourer in a uranium mine, I was hit by a large chunk of rock. As a result I have become a hunchback for life.

Naturally, I was deeply depressed. I was in love with a girl. Would she accept me, with such a deformity? Who would want to marry a hunchback? I felt like an outcast. Little children mocked me, crying behind my back, 'Hunchback! Hunchback!'

One day a little boy stopped me on the street and asked me, 'Uncle, what is it that you are carrying on your back?' I thought, *Now I will be mocked again*. But nevertheless I replied, 'A hump'.

He looked at me with love. 'Uncle, I don't believe that. God is love, He does not give people deformities.

What you have on your back is a box containing angel wings. If you carry it with humility and love to the end of your life, the box will then open; the wings will unfold; and with those wings you will fly to a beautiful heaven.'

I wept when I heard those words. Even now I weep again, as I write these lines.

This Soviet child had within him the Holy Spirit, who in Scripture is called the Comforter, and knew how to offer a word of cheer to one in need.

We too have the promise of the same Spirit, and under His blessed influence, our words can provide comfort and encouragement.

* * *

A sick child was asked how he was feeling. He replied, 'I suffer, but I suffer little, because Jesus said, "Suffer little, children, to come unto Me." Only those who think of their sufferings as little are called.'

To this child a comma made all the difference. The earliest Greek manuscripts have no trace of punctuation. Jesus *could* have pronounced the sentence like that!

* * *

The parents of President Ronald Reagan did not practise much religion, but his grandfather did. When the family were preparing to dine with him, little Ronald's parents warned him, 'Grandfather always asks every child to recite a Bible verse at meal time. You must have one memorised.'

But the future president was only four, so his mother found him an easy verse to remember: 'Jesus wept' (John 11:35). Ronald was now sure of himself.

At dinner, with ten children sitting at the table, grandfather asked the first for a verse. 'Jesus wept,' he replied promptly.

Ronald was in despair. What was he to do now? To

make matters worse, his mother had not been the only one to find a simple solution to the problem. Two other children produced the same verse, and grandfather eyed them with displeasure. Ronald shrank in his chair.

When his turn came, however, he had a sudden inspiration. 'Jesus weeps,' he volunteered.

The other children laughed. Grandfather rebuked him: 'That is not written in the Bible!'

Ronald defended himself. 'It may not be written, but it is true.'

Grandfather was unrelenting: 'Jesus wept then because He was at the tomb of a friend. Why would He weep now?'

'He weeps now,' said Ronald, 'because we children only know that He wept a long time ago.'

That was a remarkable insight for a child. The Bible teaches that we are involved with a God who is *crushed* because of our adulterous hearts (Ezek. 6:9, NKJV). Our Lord is also wearied (Mal. 2:17). When on earth, He was a man of sorrows acquainted with grief. As such, He represented the heart of God (cf. John 14:9).

At the age of thirty He was told that He looked around fifty (John 8:57). So much sorrow was visible on His face that some believed He was suicidal, and asked 'Will He kill Himself?' (John 8:22). That is not a question that is asked of somebody who looks cheerful and happy.

It is part of children's theology to seek God's sadness, and to want to make Him rejoice with singing (Zeph. 3:17).

*   *   *

A four-year-old in an American department store was given several biscuits, among them one shaped like the United States. His mother asked, 'What does this remind you of?'

'I know!' he replied, beaming. 'It's the weather.' It had reminded him of the television satellite picture of the United States on the evening news.

Does the name 'Jesus' remind us of the real Jesus, of the whole Jesus; or does it only remind us of something associated with that name?

* * *

As a pastor in Rumania during the war, I had only one suit, which eventually became worn and frayed. I had to get a new one.

One morning in our family devotions, we read these words: 'The man with two tunics should share with him who has none' (Luke 3:11).

Mihai, who was then four, interrupted. 'You've got two suits now. You should give one to Brother X, who is in rags.'

'Which one should I give him?' I asked.

'The new one, of course. God always gives the best.'

It was a difficult decision, but I took his words as a mandate, and the God who gives generously somehow kept me clothed.

* * *

On her first visit to a church with stained glass windows, a little girl asked her mother who the persons were, through whom the sun shone.

'They are saints,' her mother replied.

She thought about this for a while, then said: 'Now I understand what being a saint means. It means, to be a girl through whom Jesus's beauty shines, even if I'm not beautiful myself.'

When one reads the sad biographies and dark episodes in the lives of some saints, this childish definition becomes astonishingly perceptive and true.

* * *

At our family devotions, we read the song of the virgin Mary which is known as the *'Magnificat'*. Then I said, 'Let us pray.'

Amelie, then five, spoke up. 'Isn't what we just read a prayer? We weren't just reading.'

In her childish thinking she had followed the Scripture prayerfully. There was no need to begin to pray after the reading!

No wonder Jesus said, 'Unless you change and become like little children, you will never enter the kingdom of heaven' (Matt. 18:3).

*   *   *

Misinterpretations

"In due course a tree will grow."

A father wishing to put his son to the test gave him a pound coin and a ten-pence piece for the Sunday school collection. 'Put whichever of the two you want to in the offering,' he said. 'It's your choice.'

When the boy returned he said to his father, 'I listened to the pastor's advice – and I gave the ten-pence piece.'

'Is that what the pastor really said?'

'He certainly did! He said we should give cheerfully,

and it was a lot easier to be cheerful giving the ten-pence piece!'

We should all give as much as we can cheerfully, but we have to learn how to give both cheerfully and with generosity.

*   *   *

In our family, before going to church on Sunday each grandchild receives from his daddy some money to put in the offering.

Five-year-old Alex once queried this. 'Why should I give money to God? Does He want to become a millionaire? Let's send Him a Bible. You told me that there's a verse in it that says, "The love of money is the root of all evil."'

God not only knows but inspired the Bible, and we need not remind Him of those words. But some pastors would do well to ponder St. Paul's comment.

I know one clergyman whose small granddaughter asked him, 'What does the word "allergy" mean?' He explained it as an aversion to certain foods or medicines. The child replied, 'I understand, Grandpa. You are allergic to money.'

If only that were true of all ministers! Too many nowadays are preoccupied with their benefits and investment and properties. Even the clergyman who told this story said that he felt that this most beautiful compliment was not entirely true of himself, though he wished it were.

*   *   *

Like many children, Amelie sometimes has a finicky appetite.

Once I said to her, 'It's not good for you to only eat dessert. You must first eat your soup and salad, and the other good things that Grandma prepares.'

She replied, 'I eat as Scripture tells me to.'

'What do you mean by that?' I inquired in surprise.

'The Bible says that God prefers the dessert! Look, here it is, read it.'

The verse she actually showed me said that God led His people forty years 'through the desert' – she had misread it as 'dessert'.

I smiled, but I could not help wondering whether perhaps we adults are not sometimes just as guilty of reading into the Bible what we hope to find there.

* * *

The English language, with its many 'homonyms' – words that sound the same but have very different meanings – can be very confusing to a young child. A five-year-old observed, 'It must be very wrong to fly in a plane. Jesus said, "Lo, I am with you always."'

Of course, he had thought it said 'low'.

We smile. But in truth, Jesus is with us only if we seek the low places. The Bible says that 'in lowliness of mind' we should value others better than ourselves (cf. Phil. 2:3).

* * *

On the other hand, Amelie once remarked that Jesus must have enjoyed flying in aeroplanes. Puzzled, I told her that He never flew. But she insisted that He did, and pointed to a heading in her Bible: 'Jesus' flight to Egypt', and to Luke 6:17 where it is said that Jesus 'stood in the plain'. As his disciples and a large multitude were with Him, she added, it must have been a large plane!

The subtleties of English spelling had not yet become apparent to her.

I was reminded of a Russian Baptist who, unlike other Baptists, insisted on making the sign of the cross. He justified himself by asserting, 'It is written in the Bible that we must do so.'

In Russian, the word *krestitsia* has two meanings: to be

baptised, and to cross oneself. He had adopted both meanings of the word.

*   *   *

Schoolchildren were asked to draw the holy family. One child drew them in an aeroplane. Four heads were looking through the windows.

Curious, the teacher asked, 'You have Jesus, Mary and Joseph – but who is the fourth person?'

'That's Pontius, the pilot!'

From the mouths of babes have come many versions of the Lord's prayer. One prayed, 'Our Father, Harold be Thy name,' and 'Give us this day our jelly bread.'

But are grown-ups any better than children?

When Jesus cried from the cross, 'Eli, Eli,' His hearers thought He was calling Elijah. How do we listen to the words of the Bible?

Jesus once asked, 'How do you read it?' (Luke 10:26).

*   *   *

A child who heard that God Himself wrote the Ten Commandments on tablets of stone observed, 'God must write with His left hand.'

'Why do you say that?'

'Well, you read to me yesterday from the Bible, that Jesus sits on God's right hand – so He can't move it.'

To an adult this is an entertaining deduction, but it is also a correct guess. The Law comes from the side of harshness, called in the Bible the left side; whereas grace flows from the right side (cf. Matt. 25:33). The saved are on His right.

*   *   *

Some children might have theological intuitions, but since they are human and influenced by the good and evil to which they are exposed, it is our responsibility to be careful what we say in their presence.

A teacher asked in class, 'Is the world round?'

Isaac replied, 'No, Ma'am.'

'Is it flat, then?'

'No, Ma'am.'

'Well,' demanded the teacher, 'if it is neither round nor flat, what is it?'

Isaac was equal to the challenge: 'My Papa says it's crooked.'

*   *   *

Another child was asked, 'Where do you live?'

'In hell,' was the startling reply.

Next he was asked, 'Who is your father?'

'The devil.'

The teacher was shocked. 'How can you say such things?'

'It's what my mother says, all the time.'

Children can receive negative images from us – of the world, mankind, the Church, clergy, rulers, our nation.

If they do, we will be held responsible for their negative or false theology.

It is wrong to criticise churches, clergy or grown-ups in the presence of children.

*   *   *

During World War II, a child in an American home heard only the worst about Germans from the tender age of two. Since there was no television, the child could not possibly understand what a 'German' actually was.

But once her mother warned her, 'Be careful; there are germs on the plate.' Now she knew. When her father came into the room, she announced, 'I've got Germans on my plate!'

Be careful of what you tell children. If you stir up disgust in them for a certain category of men, they may unintentionally project it on to others who are related to them perhaps only by a syllable.

*   *   *

At the age of six, Amelie was more charitable towards sinners than were most of her elders. 'I don't believe there is a hell,' she said. 'Bad men enter Paradise as well – but with a sad heart.'

Concerning the existence of hell, there has been much debate. Is it a place, or simply a horrible state of mind experienced by those eaten with remorse, with no hope of reparation or restoration?

When St. John Chrysostom was asked which of the two he thought was true, he answered, 'I don't speculate about hell. I shun it!'

* * *

At seven, Amelie approached me one day and asked me to baptise her dog.

'Honey, only humans are baptised, not dogs.'

'Why?'

'Because dogs can't tell the difference between good and evil. They are not responsible.'

She was thrilled. 'If my dog has no sin, then it will surely be with me in the resurrection!'

Does not Isaiah 11 describe the messianic kingdom as belonging also to sheep and tame wolves, which will be led by a little child?

* * *

Children's questions are sometimes perceptive, and sometimes foolish and perplexing. Amelie once stumped me with: 'Grandpa, why don't you bow to windows?'

'Wherever does the Bible say such a foolish thing?'

She promptly showed me: 'Honour widows.' With her limited vocabulary and experience – she knew nothing about widows – she had given the printer the benefit of the doubt and supplied the 'missing' letter. She wanted to fulfil a commandment which she thought she had found in the Bible, even though it made absolutely no sense.

When it comes to fulfilling God's commands – do we lean on our own understanding?

Jewish theology distinguishes between *mitzvah*, a commandment that is intelligible, and *chok*, a commandment for which we can see no reason but which must be fulfilled because God says so.

* * *

Members of a family were discussing the Christmas story. The mother asked the others why they thought Jesus was born in a stable.

Seven-year-old John answered, 'Because there weren't any doctors at that time.'

'But,' countered his mother, 'God could have provided a nice place for Him to be born in if He had wanted to.'

'Well,' reasoned John, 'God was in Mary's tummy, and He couldn't work out anything from there.'

We know of no high thoughts or great deeds on Jesus' part while He was in Mary's womb. Some keep Him locked up in a closet, and then wonder why he does not perform miracles.

* * *

Eight-year-old Amelie confided one day, 'I love a boy who is in my class, and I told him so.'

'What did he say?'

'He said he couldn't stand me, and he hit me on the head as well.'

'Well then, you had a chance to obey Jesus' advice to respond with love!'

'But Jesus told us to turn the other cheek when somebody hits you on the *cheek*. He didn't say what to do when somebody hits you on the head. So I did the same thing to him, and now he won't forget me.'

Children, like us, have a tendency to pharisaism. They also have their own excuses for evading the universal duty of love, which applies in all circumstances when there is no specific commandment covering an unexpected situation.

* * *

A boy of six saw a skeleton for the first time and wanted to know what it was.

'Those are the bones of a man who has died,' he was told.

'Oh,' he commented, with childish logic, 'so it's just the fat that goes to heaven!'

In this case the child was wrong in his theology. Fat can be an impediment to entering heaven: 'Small is the gate and narrow the road that leads to life' (Matt. 7:14). Delicacies and luxuries must be left to others if we are to advance along that narrow way.

* * *

A Baptist child in America was baptised at the early age of six, on a particularly cold day. Next day he sang with his family the hymn 'Holy, holy, holy', which ends with the words, 'God in three persons'. The child sang, 'God in four persons.'

When he was chided for this, he said, 'But I was baptised in the names of four persons. When the pastor immersed me, he said "In the name of the Father – Brr! – the Son – Brrr! – and the Holy Spirit – Brrr!"'

The pastor had shivered aloud, and the child, too overwhelmed by emotion to register the chill of the water, had assumed that 'Brrr' was the name of a fourth member of the Trinity.

In Communist countries, where the underground Church has no baptistries, believers in winter make holes in the ice through which to baptise.

In Western countries, we should not only count our blessings, but also ignore our inconveniences.

* * *

During family devotions a child heard that we are made of dust and, when we die, return to dust. A little later he commented, 'There's a man under my bed who's either being born or dying.'

'What do you mean?' queried his startled mother.

'There's a lot of dust under my bed!'

*   *   *

Another child was taught that Adam became a living soul when God breathed His spirit into him. He sighed: 'So God is dead.'

The child could not be convinced otherwise: 'Anyone who gives up his spirit is dead,' he explained.

*   *   *

At five, Mihai asked me where apricot trees come from. I told him, 'You have to dig a hole in the ground, put an apricot stone in it, cover it and then water it. In due course a tree will grow.'

Excitedly he summoned his brother and together they followed my instructions. After watering their buried treasure, they dug it up again immediately to see whether a tree had begun to grow. Naturally, they were greatly disappointed.

Children in this respect make the same mistakes as adults. We all rush to see results. God made the world in six days, not one.

*   *   *

When I read to Mihai from the book of Joshua, about how God ordered wars, his comment was, 'This must have been before God repented and became a Christian.'

Christians should take care not to read the writings of the Old Testament undiscerningly.

*   *   *

Children, it seems, sometimes know only too well how to be deceitful.

A Slovak nun, a primary school teacher, tells of an amusing incident. She was distributing sweets to the children on St. Nicholas' day. One child, Stanko, was ill, so she gave a slipper full of sweets to another boy, John, to take to him.

When Stanko was better, she asked him if he had enjoyed the present. He claimed that he had never received it. So she decided to confront the two boys.

'I gave them to you,' said John, pointing to himself.

'I didn't get anything,' protested Stanko.

But John, pointing to himself again, repeated, 'I gave them to *you*. Don't you call me "you", when you speak to me? Well then, I gave them to "you". I carried out my assignment.'

Once I had to speak to an American pastor about his financial dealings, which were not above board. He said, 'You don't understand the Bible at all. All money belongs to God. I am God's child. What's wrong with depositing God's money in the bank account of one of His beloved children? We Christians all belong to one body. It only *seems* that I have dishonestly taken for myself something that belongs to another. We are one; the money belonged to a member of the body; and after I have taken it, continues to be the property of the same body – though of another member.'

Such deceptions are amusing in children, but in adults they are criminal.

As we seek to become like little children in matters of faith, let us at the same time remember that all of us, children as well as adults, have sinned. We do well to shun childish foibles, while emulating childlike faith.

* * *

The greatest danger in children's theology lies in the fact that they are prone to gullibility. Because of their trusting nature, they are easily led astray. The suggestibility of all human beings is limitless, but it is greatest in children.

Two small boys were discussing the myth of Icarus.

'There was once a prisoner who wanted to escape. He stuck some feathers on himself with wax and flew. But he went so near the sun that the wax melted, the feathers fell off and he fell into the sea!'

'Is that a true story?'

'Of course it's true! It's in my history book.'

Another boy was a member of the Orthodox Church; he was sure that St. George really did kill a dragon, because he had seen ikons portraying the victory.

We can learn a great deal from children, but let us grow in understanding and not be taken in by every wind of doctrine, nor be led astray from the truth and go after fables (cf. 1 Tim. 4). Furthermore, let us not demand of our pastors that they 'tell us pleasant things' (Isa. 30:10).

* * *

A child asked his father, 'Why are all the pastors in America either white or black? Why aren't there any green pastors?'

'Where did you find such a silly idea?' laughed his father.

'Daddy, you read yesterday from Psalm 23 that He leads us to green pastors.'

This urban child did not know what a pasture was, and could not relate to it.

Pastors must be very careful to communicate effectively. Even adults can misunderstand what they are told, thinking only in terms of their own theological vocabulary – obviously more limited than that of the pastor. They relate what he says to what they know.

I was born a Jew. The Christian language was completely foreign to me. When at the age of twenty-seven I entered a Christian church for the first time and heard the congregation singing of 'the lamb of God', I whispered to my wife, 'These are the idolators of old who worship animals!'

Children's misapprehensions should serve as a reminder to theologians and preachers, to speak the truth plainly. They are handling matters of eternal significance.

* * *

'God must have an awfully big stomach,' said a little boy returning from church.

'Why?' asked his mother.

'Because the Bible says, "In Him we live and move and have our being." ' (Acts 17:28).

Another boy aged four observed that God must have many ears, because He has so many prayers to listen to at once.

The Hindus paint Krishna with many arms, because God has to help many people simultaneously.

Children, and primitive religions, have sensed a truth: heavenly beings have many more organs for perceiving reality than we do.

It is written of the cherubim that 'their entire bodies, including their backs, their hands and their wings, were completely full of eyes' (Ezek. 10:12). They also have four faces, with ears, noses and mouths on each.

If this is true of His heavenly creatures, one can be sure that God is even better equipped for hearing, seeing and handling everything. Children can be reassured about God's capacity to take care of them. There is no need to worry that a prayer will go by unheard.

* * *

Versions

Back to playing with toys.

I taught little Alex the verse, 'He shall pray unto God, and He will be favourable unto him' (Job 33:26, AV). But the word 'favourable' did not exist in his six-year-old vocabulary. When he came to recite the verse, he said, 'He shall pray unto God, and God will pray unto him.'

He could not understand why his 'version' was wrong; it tallied with his experience. 'I pray to God and tell Him what I desire. Then He prays to me and tells me what He desires. I tell Him I love Him; He tells me the same thing. He prays even better than I do!'

We have a problem; we need a sense of purpose in life, something to live for. Jesus has a problem; He needs workers in His kingdom.

We pray to Him about our problems. He also speaks to us through the Bible, the Church, His special servants, an inner voice, the events of life; sometimes even visions and dreams.

Ultimately the child was right. We pray to Him, and He to us.

*   *   *

Sometimes children have unusual insights. An eight-year-old girl said, 'I wonder why all these people are talking about their experiences with Jesus? I never had an "experience". He told me to come; and I came. He said, "I will give you rest," and He gave it to me. I wonder also why they bother Jesus so much. He gave them rest; they should give Him rest, too.'

*   *   *

There are often guests in my home. The conversation ranges over many subjects. Once I and a fellow-Christian were discussing some philosophical problems. Ten-year-old Amelie was quietly playing with her toys in the same room.

I remarked, 'Every point of view is actually a "point of blindness", for it blinds you to every other point of view. If you look at the ceiling of a room, you cannot see the floor, and vice versa. If you look at the right side of the room you cannot see the left. Each point of view of a party, religion or social class diminishes your ability to see with equal clarity a different point of view. Only an overall intuition can get at the truth.'

To our surprise, Amelie interrupted. 'Only to see the whole is still blindness. It keeps you from recognising that there is not just the whole but also the parts, which are different from each other. The "whole" is an abstraction, which means it is only part of reality. The truth comprehends all the parts and their sum, in a totality.'

Now I cannot vouch for the fact that these were her

exact words, as I had no tape recorder running. But the thought here expressed was very definitely hers.

Everyone in the room was stunned for a moment. Amelie went back to playing with her dolls.

A multitude of Christians are now so enamoured of ecumenism that they can see only the whole as the representation of true Christianity. But individual denominations are as legitimate a part of the truth as is the sum total of which they are part – and even that statement assumes that an organic whole is a possibility and that it would be recognised as such.

Let us pursue Jesus' desire that all Christians should be one. Let us also value the certain truth that we have in our own denominations. Christianity would not have denominations were it not for the good of those who love God, though we do not yet understand the mystery that lies behind it.

But a child understood.

* * *

A six-year-old girl had heard the story of the annunciation of Mary, and asked her father, 'What is a virgin?'

He replied, 'It's a kind of forest. Look at these pictures of virgin forests in the Amazon. They are forests never penetrated by man.'

'Oh!' exclaimed the girl. 'Then the angel saw her as a virgin, alone in such a forest with no man ever to hug her. So he came to spend an hour with her and tell her beautiful things. Angels are *neat!*'

* * *

Five-year-old Alex thoughtfully remarked, 'God will have to be patient with me when I become an angel. I won't be able to fly very well. I expect it is like skating – you fall over a lot before you get good at it.'

Later he wondered, 'Aren't fallen angels merely angels who are just starting out?'

The point about fallen angels is of course far-fetched.

But Christians begin angel-like lives here on earth. Like children, they should not be discouraged if they do not become instant flying experts! It takes a great deal of practice to develop spiritual as well as physical skills.

*   *   *

When Mihai was six, I attempted to impress upon his young mind the truth of John 3:16, that God gave His only Son to die for us.

'Isn't it wonderful?' I asked, and was taken aback when he calmly replied, 'Not at all.'

I was surprised, and insisted that he explain what he meant, and he readily did so. 'It is wonderful when a poor man gives a large gift to the Church. But large gifts are normal for a rich man. For God, it must be the normal thing to give the best.'

Since we belong to God's family, it should be normal for us to give of our best too.

*   *   *

A child of five, on hearing the Christmas story, commented, 'See what the angel wants you to understand. The news of Jesus' birth was a great joy only to people. For the angels, it was a great sadness. They were going to be without Him for a long time.'

May we too always be aware of how angels feel about what happens to us! Sin gives us pleasure; if it did not, we would never sin. But it grieves the angels.

*   *   *

An eleven-year-old boy once acted the role of Joseph, Jesus's adoptive father, in a Sunday school Christmas production. When he discussed with his parents what sort of shoes he should wear, they suggested sandals. He wanted cowboy boots. When his father explained that it was unlikely that Joseph would have worn cowboy boots, the boy replied, 'Yes, but he didn't have braces on his teeth, either!'

He had understood that biblical personalities can be represented in a contemporary way.

Some believers do not accept this. A lady once said to me, 'My daughter claims to be a believer, but she is not born again. Look how short her dress is – and how bare her arms!'

I pointed to the picture of her mother that hung on the wall. It was taken in the last century. The lady wore a dress as long as a nun's habit.

'What you yourself are wearing,' I pointed out, 'would have seemed like a mini-skirt to your mother. You have to accept the fact that your children may hold to the same faith as you do, but in forms other than those to which you are accustomed.'

*   *   *

The twelve-year-old son of a doctor learned in Sunday school that Jesus was delivered up to death out of envy (cf. Matt. 27:18). When he was asked why Jesus was crucified, he replied, 'Well, in the Bible it says it was because of envy. Doctors were mad at Him because He healed people for nothing. If there were many like Him, my father would be broke.'

A pastor's son contributed, 'He also deprived priests of their income by forgiving the sins of men who had not brought a sacrifice. Was Jesus right to take away the jobs of men like that?'

Albert Schweitzer, like many hundreds of self-sacrificing physicians, did not use his medical knowledge as a means of making money. On the contrary, he served the poor while remaining in poverty himself. Likewise, many pastors have been more concerned about preaching the gospel and ministering to others, than about looking for high salaries and personal well-being.

*   *   *

Somebody asked a child what it is like when you die. 'When you die,' he replied, 'God takes care of you, just like your mother did when you were alive – except God doesn't yell at you all the time.'

Ought we not to make sure that children do not see such a contrast between God and ourselves?

God is perfect. Since we are Christians, children cannot see why we are not perfect too. Jesus said, 'Be ye perfect, even as your Father in heaven is perfect' – perfect in this respect at least, that we do not yell at our children.

*　　　*　　　*

During the Nazi era, a great many members of my family were killed for the crime of being Jewish. When the slaughter began, Mihai was only two. He grew up in our home, constantly hearing conversation about killing. It seemed that whoever entered our home spoke only about relatives and acquaintances who had been murdered. The concept of actual killing was as familiar to Mihai as toy soldiers and toy wars were to other children.

One evening, after we had prayed together before bedtime, he asked me, 'Will we be killed too?'

He was only four.

I replied, 'Possibly.'

'How will it happen?'

'The police will come and take us away in a car,' I explained.

Mihai had never been in a car. In Eastern Europe pastors had no money for bus fares, let alone for cars. He rejoiced. 'And will they drive us around much?'

'Quite a lot; to the edge of town.'

'And then what?'

'And then they will shoot us all with a machine gun.'

He was silent for a few moments. Then he said earnestly, 'They will kill us a *little*, and then we will be resurrected *much* – and we will go to heaven. The police cannot follow us there because they don't know about the ladder that reaches up to the sky.'

*　　　*　　　*

The Soviet Baptist Peters was killed while transporting Bibles which had been printed in secret. As his wife wept, their four-year-old child asked, 'Mother, is heaven a very bad, ugly place?'

'What makes you ask such a foolish question?'

'I can't understand why you're crying, now that Daddy has gone to a place like Paradise, which you both always told me was lovely.'

Compare what these children say with the words of a pastor I read about. He was asked at a party, 'Can one be *sure*? Where *do* you go, Pastor, when you die?'

'To heaven, of course,' replied the pastor. 'But why should we talk about such a sad subject as death?'

For a Christian, 'death' is quite the wrong word. It means passing to a much better life. 'He is not the God of the dead, but of the living' (Matt. 22:32).

Often children do not 'put the lid on' the dead, but speak of them as if they were still living.

Alex once prayed at the meal table, 'God, thank you for the food. Please feed those in heaven also, especially General Eisenhower and George Washington.'

At the age of eight Amelie prayed for a multitude of friends – and also for the well-being of St. Paul. I asked her why. She answered, 'Paul finishes an epistle by saying "Pray for us," and that includes the other apostles. Mustn't we obey everything in the Bible? It doesn't say anywhere that we must stop praying for them when they die.'

*　　*　　*

A family had moved into a new house which was far more luxurious than the one they had lived in previously. The child wandered round admiring all the new and different things, and finally exclaimed, "What beautiful things we have now!' He would never have thought to say to his father, 'These beautiful things belong to you.'

The child understood what the Bible says: '*All things are yours* . . . and you are of Christ' (1 Cor. 3:21, 23).

*   *   *

In Russia, schoolchildren are taught that man has descended from apes.

A child stood up and said, 'Thank you, teacher, for giving us this explanation. I always wondered how Communists could be so wicked. I never knew but now you have made it clear. You are wicked because you come from gorillas.'

Another child in Russia reacted differently when told of his alleged descent: 'That can't be true. I've seen apes in the zoo and they're delightful creatures. It is a pleasure to see them jumping around, they grin at children, they are grateful if you give them a nut. I can't believe that wicked Communists could have descended from such happy creatures as apes.'

*   *   *

Rumania is an Orthodox country. In such countries it is the custom for the priest to go from house to house with a cross in his hand, blessing the family, on the first day of every month.

Little four-year-old Gaby was stopped by a priest in the street. He held out the cross towards her so that she could kiss it.

Looking up at him gravely, she asked, 'Why should I kiss it? The cross doesn't need my love. *You* do.' Whereupon she reached up, grabbed hold of the priest's beard, pulled his face down to hers, and kissed him right on the mouth.

The words might have seemed impolite, the gesture forward. But oh! If we could lavish on our fellow human beings the love we show for mere things, how much brighter this world would be! I know many Christians who are attentive to the words of Scripture, but deaf to the heart-cries of those around them.

It is not the cross, but the Man of the cross who needs our love. And Jesus said in effect, 'Inasmuch as you have shown love to your fellow man, you have shown it to Me.'

The child was right.

* * *

When he was five, Mihai said to me, 'Father, I was smarter than you! When you were young you sinned and then later you repented. I was born a Christian from the very beginning.'

A professor of religion once asked his class, 'How many of you were born Christians?' Several hands went up. He smiled tolerantly, then commented, 'No, you weren't. You were born miserable sinners like all the rest of us.'

We are not born sinning, but we are born sinners; we need the grace of God to enable us to become Christians. Through dedicated Christian parents, this grace can be mediated to children at a tender age.

In this regard, Mihai had not been smarter than me!

* * *

Amelie wanted to know how Jonah managed to get out of the fish.

Alex, with the confidence of a six-year-old, had an explanation: 'Jonah was a prophet – that means he was smart. When he boarded the ship he knew that ships sometimes sink and that he might then be swallowed by a fish. So to be on the safe side he put some red pepper in his pocket. He put the pepper in the fish's nose and that made it sneeze. Then he could slip out.'

We smile leniently at the naivety of a child, but how prepared are we for emergencies? More to the point – do we arm ourselves daily for the battle with evil? The Bible describes in precise detail the armour that will help the Christian to cope (cf. Eph. 6:13–17).

* * *

At seven Alex loved football, and tried to explain it to his Grandpa – who was not really interested: 'During the game it sometimes seems that your team is losing, but in the final minutes the game can turn and you can finish up as the winner. It's the same in the game between God and the devil. On Good Friday it seemed that God had lost. Jesus had died on the cross. But then God turned things round, and on Easter Sunday He put the ball in the devil's goal! God came out the winner.'

Let us never say 'We have lost' or 'We are lost'. The Referee has not yet blown the final whistle.

* * *

Six-year-old Alex was much impressed by a film about chivalry.

'When I'm big I'll be a knight,' he decided. 'Then I'll have to fall in love with a lady. But Grandpa, don't be frightened. When you fall in love, you don't fall down and break your bones. You fall up!'

* * *

A small boy once said something to another which he had probably heard from his parents: 'Your God is evil.' Such words never come from the heart of a child.

The young Christian replied, 'Really? Then let's work together to make Him good.'

'That's stupid. We can't decide how God should be.'

The Christian child (who was perhaps eight years old) said, 'Sure we can. God was once a boy like you and me, in the house of Joseph and Mary. They taught Him every day by word and example to be loving, good, honest and hard-working. If Jesus had been born in some other home, wicked parents might have taught Him swearing, lying, stealing and drinking. We can teach God.'

This was a child's way of expressing thoughts which are too profound for words.

The Bible says that we can 'magnify' God – which means, to make Him bigger. Bigger in what? We can make Him rejoice with singing (Zeph. 3:17). We can make Him very sad. We can provoke Him to wrath. We *can* decide how God should be. God is love – but so much depends on our response.

*   *   *

Reactions

Little Alex injured himself
climbing a fence.

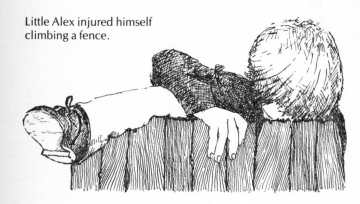

A child, who was expelled from Sunday school for being naughty, cried, 'I want my money back!'

I once did the same. I was at a Sunday morning service in a church in Boston, Massachusetts. The customary offering was taken, and I put some money on the plate. Then the pastor preached a sermon against Richard Nixon.

Though I had not voted for Nixon, I was not at all disposed to sit through a sermon against him in the morning worship hour. I bore with the minister for some ten minutes, then stood up and interrupted him: 'Please start speaking about God' (he had mentioned neither God nor Christ).

The pastor was unnerved, and shouted back, 'I have the right to say what I like.'

I replied, 'Not so, sir! When I ask for cheese at a grocer's, I get cheese; if I ask for tomatoes I get tomatoes. The store belongs to somebody else but because I am paying, I am considered the boss. I've paid here, too. I put money in the offering plate on the assumption that I would get my money's worth of knowledge about God. If you want to talk about Richard Nixon that's all right by me, but then please give me my money back.'

I had applied the principle of children's theology. If there were more children in the churches, pastors would have to give proper value, or go broke!

* * *

We were walking in a park with Mihai, who was probably four years old at the time. At one point he had to be taken to a public lavatory. As he left he said, 'The lady in charge is a very good Christian. She allows people to make her home smelly. She couldn't be nicer.'

What a beautiful image of a Christian, who is friendly and hospitable even to those he finds repulsive! He remembers that Jesus showed compassion for the poor, the unlovely, the weak; and that He invites to His banquet those from the byways as well as the highways.

* * *

When Mihai was small I once spanked him for some minor transgression. 'If you beat me again,' he told me, 'I might die. How sad you will be then!' He was genuinely not thinking about his own discomfort, but about my sadness.

I was deeply moved.

When I myself was later passing through great suffering, I surprised myself by saying the same words to God, echoing those of Job: 'You will search for me, but I will be no more' (Job 7:21).

When somebody wrongs us, we would do well to disregard our own afflictions and think rather of the harm our adversary does to himself, and of his future regrets.

* * *

At the end of World War II, posters were displayed in all the trams and buses, portraying hanged men. It was effective propaganda for capital punishment of war criminals.

One day, travelling in a tram with Mihai, I noticed that he kept his eyes covered with his hand the whole time. When I asked him why he did so, he replied, 'I don't want to look at evil.'

It is recorded that Jesus knew no evil. It is far better to have no knowledge of evil, than to know it and reject it.

*   *   *

When Mihai was five, I rebuked him for a sin. 'God has a book, and in that book there is a page with your name on it. There He writes down all your sins. There was one the day before yesterday, another yesterday, and now you have sinned again.'

He replied, 'Do you believe that God only writes down the bad things I do? Doesn't He write down the good things as well?'

He was right. The image of God as a policeman who books one only for law-breaking is wrong – and harmful.

*   *   *

A child was given two coins, one for himself, the other for the offering in Sunday school. Clutching them in his hand, he trudged off to church. On the way he fell over, dropped the coins, and could only find one of them again.

'I'm sorry, God,' he said, 'but your coin is missing.'

Children can sometimes be selfish – just like their parents!

*   *   *

When Mihai was small he could not be dissuaded from coming with us to all-night vigils, though he sometimes fell asleep half-way through them.

He would complain that the services were too short.

He often said, 'Being in church is being with God, so why not spend all our lives there? The church should be our playground.'

He certainly acted as if it were, and could not understand why everyone was so serious in church.

One Sunday morning he disrupted the whole service with his noisy playing. By the time we got home I had decided to punish him.

'Do you think it is nice that only the pastor's son misbehaves in church?' I demanded.

He replied, 'You think I wasn't listening to the sermon. But I know every word of it.'

'Very well; what was it about?'

'You spoke enthusiastically about forgiving somebody who has sinned,' he replied. 'So you ought to do that now.'

There could be no arguing with such words!

* * *

Almost since the day she was born, Amelie has heard stories about Jesus. I have sometimes wondered what the name could mean to a very small child, to whom so much remains yet to be told.

When she was two, I showed her a picture of Jesus for the first time, and pronounced His name, pointing to His bleeding heart. She became very serious, and spontaneously kissed the picture twice, though she had never seen anyone do such a thing.

Even at that early age, she knew that Jesus was a person to be cherished.

Speak to babies about Jesus. Speak in their presence about His glory! One cannot tell how early their understanding begins.

* * *

When Amelie was three my wife gave her a sweet. The child took another piece from the box and gave it to me.

Gently refusing it, I explained, 'Today is Friday. This is a day on which we do not eat.'

Of course, she asked why. I told her what fasting is, and explained that it is an old Christian custom not to eat on Friday, the day on which Jesus was crucified. (This fast is particularly observed by the persecuted Church.)

Amelie gave both sweets back to her grandmother, saying, 'I will fast too.'

*   *   *

A boy wrote God a note: 'Dear God, church is all right, only the services are very boring. Can you write some new songs? Your friend, Barry.'

True religion is never boring, because its focus is on a lovely person. The psalmist wrote, 'Sing to the Lord a new song' (Psa. 149:1).

*   *   *

Dorothy, a girl of six, protested when her mother insisted on treating her doll Elizabeth just as a doll.

'She's not a doll; she's a *girl*. I can tell. If she were a doll I would not put her nappy on, so you see – she's not a doll.'

The way I treat a person affects how I think about him. If I treat him badly I will begin to think of him as an enemy.

If we get into the habit of following a false god, we begin to think of it as real because we worship it. That is how false religions begin. That is how the nightmare of Jonestown started.

We should become like little children in matters of faith and trust, but not in everything. Our powers of reason and discernment must mature.

*   *   *

Somebody asked a minister's nine-year-old son, 'Have you decided what to be when you are grown-up? Will you be a pastor like your father?'

He answered, 'I don't think so. Ministers work too much and don't get paid much. My father could have made more money as a plumber.'

Another boy of six was invited to dinner along with his parents. During the meal, he announced loudly to the hostess: 'You sure don't know how to cook!'

Jesus tells us to become like little children, honest and forthright – but not naughty and mean-spirited. The truth should always be seasoned with politeness and kindness.

* * *

One of my nieces had several guests at a time when her husband was abroad. Being short of accommodation, she explained to Alex, then five years old, 'You'll have to sleep with me in my bed.'

'I can't do that,' protested Alex. 'We're not married!'

Would that those who are much older had such strong principles!

Valladares, the Christian poet, spent twenty-two years in Cuban jails. In prison, he was married. On his release friends prepared a bedroom for the couple, who had not yet enjoyed the privileges of their relationship.

'I cannot sleep with her yet,' he said gently. 'We only had a civil marriage. I will wait for the religious ceremony.'

He and Alex shared the same theology.

* * *

My son and daughter-in-law once took the children to a restaurant that was not very impressive from the outside. Alex asked his father, 'Why are you taking us to such a shabby place?'

But once inside, they saw that everything was clean and pleasant.

Alex asked to be allowed to say grace. 'I thank You, God,' he said with childish candour, 'for the lesson You taught me today, that I should not call somebody or something ugly because of its outward looks. Help me always to see the inside.'

Man sees not as God sees, for God looks at the heart. Let us not be hasty in our judgements.

*   *   *

Victor, a Jewish child of five, was being driven past a church. 'Father, let's stop here a while and see how God is today.'

Do we go to church with such a purpose?

Victor also took part in a Christian prayer meeting, in which every prayer began with 'Lord Jesus . . .' Puzzled, he asked, 'Where is God in your prayers?' It was a valid question; Jesus taught us to pray 'Our Father', and to approach the Father 'in My name'. He never taught us to pray to Himself.

*   *   *

A twelve-year-old Jewish child was told the story of Jesus and was warned, 'Know that if all those things are true, and you don't believe them, you will perish.' He replied to the teacher, 'Know by the same token, sir; you will perish if those things are untrue and you have believed them.'

We all need to ask the age-old question, 'What is truth?' However, unlike Pilate, we should follow it through and not rest until we have found out the answer.

But the primary question should be, '*Who* is truth?' Jesus said simply, 'I am the truth' (cf. John 14:6). Having settled that, we next learn 'Your word is truth' (John 17:17). The Jewish boy had no need to remain in doubt.

We must take care as to what we believe or disbelieve. We walk a narrow pathway to heaven.

*   *   *

A child, on being shown the splendid mausoleum of a millionaire, exclaimed, 'This is *really* living!'

*   *   *

Alex, who has been in many prosperous homes, remarked 'It isn't good to be a millionaire. It makes you nervous, and then you don't share with people.'

*   *   *

A husband and wife quarrelled constantly, and finally decided to get a divorce. On hearing this, their six-year-old child – who had been a constant witness of their disputes – said, 'I can't tear myself in two to please you.'

Next morning he told his parents, 'My shoulders and arms are aching. During the night I felt like Daddy was pulling me by one arm and Mummy by the other. I feel as if I've been torn in pieces and I don't know how to put them back together again.'

God Himself has put into children's hearts the intuition that 'What God has joined together, men should not separate.'

*   *   *

In Russia, secondary school pupils are taken to the Museum of Atheism in Moscow.

A guide showed one school group all the exhibits designed to prove the evils of religion. They were shown pictures illustrating man's evolution from animals, the horrors of the Inquisition, and so on.

Then the guide showed them an ancient crucifix. 'You see, children, in olden times people were backward. They believed that there was a man called Jesus who was God's son. It was supposed that He came from heaven to earth, to save men from their sins. In their stupidity, they believed that He took everybody's sins upon Himself and that, animated by love, He was crucified for our misdeeds. Our forefathers had no sense! Their religion said that if anybody believed in Jesus he would be forgiven for all his sins, and would eventually be resurrected from the dead, just as Jesus Himself was resurrected, and would enjoy a beautiful life for all eternity!'

A girl of twelve began to weep.

'Comrade teacher,' she said, 'Thank you for telling us these interesting things. My wrongdoings have been greatly distressing me. I made my mother cry; I lied to my father; I cheated at school. I have been wondering how I can get rid of my sins. And I am terrified of dying. Every time I see a funeral, I think, "Some day I will be lying in a coffin, and everything will be over." But I want to live!'

She continued, 'If no modern intelligent person can believe what you have told us, then I will return to the foolish ways of our forefathers. It is better to be foolishly forgiven, and be resurrected, than to be burdened with them intelligently and miss heaven. I will always be grateful to you for what you have shown me.'

*　　*　　*

Once Amelie saw Jesus in a dream. He was saying gently, 'Come to Me.' She went to Him, circling as if in a dance.

Dreams about Jesus are rare. They may well be premonitions.

*　　*　　*

The Russian Christian, Gennhadi Malachov, had completed his prison sentence, and his family had arrived at the jail to take him home.

At the prison gate, his daughter asked, 'Father, where are you going?'

'I am coming home with you, my child.'

'No,' the girl said unexpectedly, 'you must stay here.'

'Why? Aren't you happy that we will be together again?'

'No,' replied his daughter, who had been born after his imprisonment and had never known him at home. 'I have always been taught that my Daddy's place is in jail, to suffer for Christ.'

A Christian child should know that his father is a cross-bearer, and should be surprised to see him without a cross. Jesus said, 'Take up your cross, and follow Me.' That is the role of the Christian, the 'Christ-follower'.

* * *

The child of Michel Sakharov went with his mother to visit his father in jail, where he had been imprisoned for his faith.

The prisoner stretched out his arms to the child and said, 'Come to me, darling.'

The child clung to his mother, and said, 'I don't want to go to him. My father is handsome, I've seen his pictures; this skinny wrinkled man is not my father.'

Children of Christians tortured and imprisoned by Communists are not the only ones who fail to recognise their loved ones. The Jews loved God in glory, but when the Son of God appeared first as a baby in a manger, and later as a marred and crucified Saviour, they failed to recognise Him.

Malachov's child had sharper spiritual perception than Sakharov's.

* * *

During the Christmas season a Sunday school teacher told her class about Jesus' birth in a stable. The following week one pupil asked, 'Do those poor people have a house yet?'

That is a good reaction to the Christmas story; the Holy Family should have a home. My own home should certainly be made available. Better still – my heart.

* * *

After visiting Israel for a few days at the age of eight, Amelie observed, 'This is a land where cats don't scratch, dogs don't bite, and all men are good.' After a brief and unpleasant encounter with a cat, she changed her mind.

'Some cats scratch – but they must have come from somewhere else.'

It is said that beauty is in the eye of the beholder.

Jesus taught us to look at the lilies as they grow, not after they are picked; at birds as they are fed by God, not after they are killed by predators. We are told to worship God 'in the beauty of holiness', and to think about 'whatsoever things are lovely'.

We ask God to turn away His eyes from our sins. Let us also learn to turn our eyes away from what is ugly. Let us open our eyes to the beauties of the holy land, the holy Church, the holy nation, the holy Bible.

*   *   *

Little Alex injured himself while climbing a fence. Examining his wounds, which were bleeding, he said, 'Now I know what a crucifixion is like.'

May we also bear every wound as a reminder of Jesus' sufferings on Golgotha.

*   *   *

Before our trip to Israel, I promised Amelie that I would take her to all the places that were significant in the life of Jesus: Bethlehem where He was born, Nazareth where He grew up, places in Galilee and Judea where He preached, and then the places where He was judged, whipped, crucified and entombed; finally, the place of His ascension.

She thought for a while, and then said, 'Let's do it the other way round. Show me first the place where, glorified, He ascended to heaven. Then I will not be so sad when I see the places where He suffered.'

I was reminded of meeting a Russian lieutenant during World War II. He knew absolutely nothing about Christ.

I told him the story of Jesus' birth, childhood and baptism, and then described the Sermon on the Mount, the parables and the miracles. He, who had never heard anything like it, was jubilant. Dancing round the room, he exclaimed, 'What fairy-like beauty! How could I have lived, without knowing these things?'

Then I told him how Jesus was betrayed, arrested, bound, sentenced, flogged and crucified. He could not hold back his tears. When he heard that Jesus' enemies had asked Him to show them He was the Son of God, by descending from the cross, he considered that it was a reasonable demand. He was sure I was going to say that Jesus agreed to it.

When He heard that in fact, Jesus actually died on the cross, he collapsed into an armchair and wept bitterly. He had found a Saviour – but to no avail. Jesus had died.

Only when I was able to tell him the story of the resurrection did he once again rejoice. I could have spared him the tears and anguish, if I had told him at the beginning that the story of Jesus has a happy ending.

*   *   *

Four-year-old Terry listened to a religious broadcast and heard the preacher say, 'Jesus is mine.'

'That's wrong!' he exclaimed. 'He forgot about me. Jesus is ours, not only his.'

Take all you can from Jesus and his Church, but remember that nobody has a monopoly. Jesus taught us to pray '*Our* Father', not '*My* Father'.

*   *   *

A boy who had heard me speak of 'narcissism' asked many questions about it.

Narcissism means self-admiration. Narcissus was a legendary person who spent all his time gazing at his own reflection, which was to him of surpassing interest.

The boy remarked, 'Then our Sunday school teacher is a narcissist. He boasts that man is the crown of creation. But when I went to Marineland I saw whales and dolphins doing amazing things. Can men do forty-ton backflips? Why does the Bible call Jesus a lion and a lamb?

Because the lion is more powerful and the lamb more gentle than men.'

Little children are free of adult sophistication, and they don't look down on the animal kingdom. It's true that God made only man in His image. He gave him a mind that thinks, feels and reasons. But unlike Narcissus, man is to reflect God, not himself.

*   *   *

Michel Horev, a Russian Baptist, wrote from jail the story of his conversion. His father Mihai had died a martyr's death, leaving his mother very poor and with four small children.

Once she was peeling potatoes – their only food – and asked Michel as a favour to read the Scriptures to her as she did so.

Michel baulked at that. He found the Bible boring. 'You read, and I'll peel the potatoes.'

'That's not such a good idea; I'll have to find my glasses first, which might take a while. Please be kind and read to me.'

'What part do you want to hear?' he said reluctantly.

'The Sermon on the Mount.'

Such a long passage, thought Michel. *Three long chapters.* He was a very poor reader, and his eyes were weak. He got the Bible.

'Blessed are the poor in spirit,' he began, struggling over the words. 'Blessed are those who mourn.' But suddenly his eyes were opened to words which were not on the page. *Blessed are my parents. My father suffers in chains. My mother is sad. Her life is bitter, too.*

'Blessed are the meek,' he continued. *Jesus must have meant my parents. They've always been so meek.* 'Blessed are the merciful . . .' *Mother would share her last piece of bread with anyone who was hungry or poor.* 'Blessed are the pure in heart . . .' *They've never had a spot on their hearts.* 'Blessed are the peacemakers . . .' *They don't know what hate is. If it were left to them, they would even be at peace with the Communists.*

'Blessed are those who are persecuted for righteousness' sake . . .' *For this blessing I am without a father.*

His mind flashed back to earlier days. What a strange man his father had been – as strange as this book!

His mother had told him that when he had been born, the doctor had said to Michel's parents, 'The boy's eyes seem weak. He may never see very well. You will have to accept the fact that he may soon be totally blind.'

On hearing the doctor's sombre prognosis, his father lifted the infant Michel towards heaven and said, 'Thank you, God, for giving me a son after four girls, and thank you that he has poor sight, perhaps no sight at all . . .'

His mother interrupted – 'Stop this senseless prayer!' Tears coursed down her cheeks. 'You don't give thanks for a child's blindness.'

'Do you believe, then,' replied her husband, 'that God makes mistakes? If he is blind he will be useless for factory work or for any profession. Therefore he will be dedicated to the Lord's work. The Bible can be read in Braille.'

Remembering this, Michel thought to himself, *That must be how Mary thanked God for giving her a Son whom the prophets described as a 'man of sorrows', destined to die on a cross.*

'Rejoice, and be exceeding glad . . .' He read on and on, through page after page of the Sermon on the Mount. By the time he had finished, he had settled in his heart that he belonged to Jesus.

His father's predictions came true. He really did become a pastor, and as a result he too has been in prison for many years. He is in prison as I write, and he is almost blind.

*   *   *

In Aurora, Colorado, USA, an eight-year-old boy named Charlie hanged himself.

He had sometimes been mischievous. Once he deliberately ruined school equipment belonging to other pupils. As a punishment his mother told him she would withhold his pocket money to pay for the damaged articles.

He became resentful. 'When I'm naughty I have to lose my pocket money, but when my parents have a big quarrel and they are naughty God does not keep back their pocket money.' His final argument was suicide at the age of eight.

Charlie's brother told his grandmother, 'Charlie went to heaven to visit God, but he'll be back in a couple of weeks.'

No doubt, when Jesus returns, Charlie will be back, together with all who have suffered innocently. Will we be able to look into their reproachful eyes?[1]

Parents, teachers and judges often have to punish wrongdoing, and in this they are the representatives of God, who hates sin. Everyone who punishes must take good care to be very God-like, lest those who are punished be driven to despair. Unjust punishment inflicted by unrighteous men can produce indelible trauma, neurosis or psychosis.

Biographers tell us that one beating received by the young Lenin caused him to tear the cross from his neck and become a God-hater for life. His father had asked a priest what he should do with his son, who had failed to attend church. The priest replied, 'Beat him and beat him.' The boy overheard.

One slap received by Tito when he was an altar-boy made him a revolutionist and a mass-murderer. Having been slack in his duties of serving the priest, he was punished with a slap he never forgot.

Many people are like Charlie. They say, 'I get punished

---

1. Story from *Denver Post*, 22 April 1985.

for my mistake, while God is good to those who beat me –
though their sins are greater than mine.'

Children's theology demands that adults behave as
they expect others – especially children – to behave. They
all too easily perceive the fallacy of 'Do as I say, not as I
do.'

Jesus said, 'If you love Me, keep My commandments' –
but He kept them too.

* * *

Some boys were misbehaving. Their Sunday School
teacher wished to impress on them the fact that God
would judge them. So he lectured them at length, repeating over and over again, 'Where is God? I say, where is
God?'

One boy whispered uneasily to another, 'Let's get out
of here – we're getting blamed for so many things, next
he's going to say it's our fault that God's disappeared.'

Of course children should be taught to be aware of
their sinfulness – but there is a need for proportion in all
things! We must not make them feel responsible for all
the tragedies of their homes and the world at large.

They have been born into a world that is full of sins
they did not commit. The entire weight of sin has been
carried by Jesus. It should not burden a child's heart.

* * *

In Sunday School the pastor was describing the crucifixion and death of Jesus. A child said afterwards, 'That
story can't be true!'

'Why?' responded the pastor.

'If it were true,' the child replied, 'you would have
tears in your eyes as you told it.'

Such incidents taught me how to preach.

* * *

A boy whose mother was dying at Christmas time went
into the church and took the figure of the baby Jesus out

of the crib. On the way home, he said to the figure, 'Now you can see what it's like not having your mother.' When his mother recovered, he put the child Jesus back.

We can have childlike daring in our relationship with God. Who could not forgive a child?

*   *   *

Motives

"Oh, but others see my kite!
It gives them joy."

When Mihai was only five, I came home one evening to find him very distressed. He had been playing with an electric wire and had received a shock. To teach him a lesson the baby-sitter had told him, 'Now you will die.' Mihai believed her, and told me the sad story. Trying to reassure him, I said, 'Don't worry – if you die, you will go to heaven.'

'Yes,' he said, 'but I want to stay here, to do more good deeds.'

St. Paul once wrote that he wanted to depart and be with Christ 'which is better by far; but it is more necessary for you that I remain in the body' (Phil. 1:23–24).

Was Mihai speaking out of altruistic motives like Paul, or did he simply want to get out of an embarrassing situation? I can't tell.

I was similarly unsure of eleven-year-old Amelie's motives when she badly wanted to have a horse. I told her, 'That could cost a fortune! You could do a good deed by giving up what you want, and giving the money to the poor.'

'But that's what I want it for!' she explained. 'So many people beat horses. This horse might even be bought by a circus, where it would suffer terribly learning the tricks it would have to perform. If I had it to look after, the horse would have a very good life.'

Do we make our decisions out of pure motives? Are the good intentions we claim genuine?

*   *   *

There is more than a touch of irony in the story of the atheist's child who said to his parents, 'It's safer not to tell God that we don't believe in Him. Then He might take us to heaven anyway.'

*   *   *

When Amelie was tiny, someone told her the story of Lourdes. To my surprise, she insisted that I take her there.

'Why?' I asked. 'You aren't ill.'

'But I want to pray at Lourdes, that I won't become ill.'

Must we wait for trouble before appealing to God to free us from it? Must we for ever fall asleep only to awaken time and time again in revivals and crusades? Or would it be wiser to pray, 'Lead us not into temptation'?

The chief concern of pastors for their flock should not be the recovery of sinners, but teaching their congregations how to vanquish sin when it first intrudes, and how not to entertain lustful or impure thoughts.

*   *   *

My wife and I once stayed with an Indian family whose five-year-old boy had just been given, for the first time in his life, a really beautiful pair of shoes. I was barefoot, because my legs were hurting.

During the meal he must have overheard the words of John the Baptist: 'He who has two tunics, let him give to him who has none.' He took off one shoe and handed it to me.

When, not realising what was happening, I made no effort to take it, he asked whether he had done something wrong; perhaps I was not a believer?

He certainly proved that *he* was a believer.

*   *   *

When he was nearly four, Alex heard his sister say, 'I'm going to be a doctor when I grow up.'

Feeling that he needed to say something about his own plans, he chimed in, 'When I'm big, I want to be a man who will make his mother happy.'

What a beautiful ambition! We would do well to copy it. We can make our heavenly Father rejoice over us with singing (Zeph. 3:17). We can make heavenly Jerusalem – which is our mother – rejoice. Even a prodigal son can make his father happy by returning home.

*   *   *

A Scottish pastor was given notice of dismissal. During his years of service, it seemed that nobody had been converted.

Moreover, he had allowed a foolish thing to happen that had scandalised the congregation. When the offering plate had been passed around, a nine-year-old boy had asked the sidesman to put the plate on the floor. Wondering what would happen, the sidesman had done so. The boy had stood on the plate. The congregation had not understood that he had given himself as an offering.

That boy was Robert Moffat, who later became a well-known missionary in Africa. His son-in-law was David Livingstone.

We can learn from this child the best kind of giving.

*　　*　　*

A missionary in Uganda in the nineteenth century told this story.

His church had a gift day, but instead of sending their gifts ahead of time for decorating the church, they brought them with them on Sunday morning. When the service was over and the missionary stood looking at the pile of gifts, he thought he heard something. Raising his head, he saw a little African girl in the aisle.

'Do you want to speak to me?' he asked.

Very timidly the girl came to the front of the church, and said, 'Please sir, I want to give something.' Putting her hand into her scanty garment she pulled out a bag. Opening it, she brought out handful after handful of silver and gold until there was a pile on the table worth more than all the other gifts put together.

The missionary said, 'You ought not to have done this. Tell me where you took the money from, and we will put it back.'

The child burst into tears. 'It's all mine!'

'It can't be!' exclaimed the missionary. 'You are much too poor.'

Then the story came out. The child had sold herself as a slave in order to be able to give money to the church.

To become self-sacrificing like God is an excellent way to find Him.

*　　*　　*

The archives of the China Inland Mission contain a letter sent over a hundred years ago to its founder, Hudson Taylor.

If you are not dead yet, I want to send you some money I have saved up to help the little boys and girls of China to love Jesus.

The Christian Mission to the Communist World received a similar letter from a boy of nine:

Mr. Wurmbrand, my mother read to me from your book, *Tortured for Christ*. I had tears in my eyes when I heard about the sufferings of Christians under the Communists.

I hope you are grand enough to accept criticism without getting offended. My Mom told me this is a sign of grandeur in a man.

We live in Rhodesia. You lead missions in many countries. Why not in ours? It was wrong of you not to think about it. Many Rhodesians would help. I'll volunteer to become your general director. It must be nice to be at the same time a general and a director and also to serve the Church. Do your generals wear uniforms like those of The Salvation Army? Please reply. Don't despise the little ones. Our angels daily see the face of God.

I replied with a four-page letter telling him what his duties as general director would be.

As a result, not he but his mother became our general director, and the nine-year-old 'missionary' became her assistant.

*   *   *

The story is often told of the six-year-old boy who was carrying another aged four. An adult asked him, 'Isn't he too heavy for you to carry?'

The reply was, 'He ain't heavy. He's my brother.'

*   *   *

Amelie remained in the house as we accompanied departing guests to the car. Within minutes she joined us, saying, 'I was afraid that if I remained alone I might do something stupid.'

People are especially prone to doing stupid things when they are on their own and unobserved. But why should they be alone? There are no loners in God's service. Christians should remain in constant fellowship with their brethren.

Amelie's comment reminded me of a quiet madman who was a member of my congregation in Bucharest, Rumania, years ago. Once, when we invited him to lunch, my wife set before him the usual knife, fork and spoon.

He said, 'Please, take the knife away. I know I am mad, so I have said to God, "Since I'm foolish I don't know what I might do if I had access to a knife." So I promised I would never hold one in my hand.'

If only all adults and mentally healthy people had such wisdom!

* * *

Many devices for rescuing individuals from alcoholism or other bad habits are often unsuccessful. I read of one method that was very successful.

A five-year-old boy said, 'Mummy, do you know what I want for Christmas more than anything else?'

Little con-man! thought his mother. *I wonder what he's after?*

The answer bowled her over. He said, 'All I want is a Mummy who doesn't smoke any more. I love you very much, and want you to live for a long time.' Then he put his chubby arms around her neck and kissed her.

She had to brush away a tear. She never smoked again.

* * *

A mother gave her son an apple. 'Share it with your brother in a Christ-like way.'

'What do you mean?'

'Give your brother the bigger half!'

Handing the apple back to her, he said, 'Why not give it to my brother and let him have the chance to share it with me in a Christ-like way!'

We smile. But it ill becomes us to pass to others the duty of being like Him.

*　　*　　*

Children can be disarmingly honest when their motives are not entirely pure.

A grammar class was asked to write a sentence containing an object. One child wrote, 'Dear lady, you are really very beautiful.'

'Thank you very much,' responded the teacher, 'but what is the object in this sentence?'

'To get a good mark,' the pupil replied candidly.

*　　*　　*

When my grandson Alex was four, I asked him for a kiss. He said, 'I can't give it yet.' After an hour, he came to me and announced: 'Now you can have the kiss.'

I asked, 'But why not earlier?'

'Because my kiss wasn't yet stuffed with enough love.'

Are our kisses always stuffed with enough love? There is nothing more saddening than a loveless kiss.

*　　*　　*

When Luke, who was nine, heard people cursing the gypsies for stealing and fortune-telling, he wanted to be taken to them so that he could share his sweets with them. He told his mother of his intention: 'When I grow up, I am going to wash the feet of gypsies, just as Jesus did. Isn't that better than complaining that people have dirty feet? Will you let me do it?'

That child died young, having lost his sight. On his

deathbed, he said: 'I would like to take all the gypsies with me to heaven.'

*   *   *

'If someone wanted to kill me,' observed Amelie, 'I would say to him, "First let me tell you the story of Jesus." If he killed me afterwards, at least I'd go to heaven.'

Her thinking was wiser than her years. Christians in Communist or Islamic countries who are brought before torturers or executioners make it their first priority to tell them about salvation through Christ. Before answering any questions from their interrogators about the underground Church, they share their faith. Then what comes, may come.

*   *   *

Isaac Feinstein was a Hebrew-Christian missionary in Rumania who was killed in the Holocaust. He left six children behind him, one of whom died at the age of nine. On her deathbed she comforted her mother: 'You have five other children. Papa is in the next world, without any of his children. It's only right that I should go to him.'

That is how easily a child who believes is able to face death.

*   *   *

A blind child was flying a kite. She was asked, 'Why are you doing that? You can't see anything.'

'Oh, but others see my kite! It gives them joy. And I have the feeling that it draws me upwards.'

*   *   *

A child asked, 'If I pray, will I get everything that I ask for?'

'Yes, but only if it is good for you.'

'Well, "all things work together for good" anyway, so I

don't have to pray for good things! Can I pray for what is bad, and get it?'

The answer is yes, it is possible. Balaam, a false prophet, was granted the fulfilment of a bad desire, but this resulted in his own destruction.

* * *

A girl named Catherine read the whole Bible, Old and New Testaments, eight times before she reached the age of twelve. Are you wondering what became of a girl like that?

She became the wife of William Booth and the co-founder of The Salvation Army.

Such a little child can lead us, by her example, into the Word, so that we too may maximise our usefulness in the kingdom of God.

* * *

Count Zinzendorf, at the age of four, was taken to an art gallery in Düsseldorf, Germany. He stood before a picture of the crucified Christ. It bore the inscription, 'This I have done for you; what are you doing for Me?'

Then and there, the little boy decided to dedicate his life to the Saviour.

He could never forget that question. While still a child he told himself, *A faith that does nothing is just babbling*.

When he was grown up, he formed the community of the Moravians, which has as its motto, 'The Saviour deserves everything'. Missionaries from the community went to Greenland, to India, to Africa.

Acknowledging the decisive influence of a picture on the life of this Christian, can we discredit the use of holy representations in worship? We use pictorial Bibles and Bible story books for the instruction of children. Perhaps art might serve to arouse the child in every adult.

Children's theology does not object to religious art.

* * *

A partially paralysed girl, who was distressing to look at, was avoided by adults and children alike. No one wanted to be subjected to her endless complaints.

Finally she realised what the problem was. She decided not to complain any more. She would tell jokes – jokes even about her own disabilities – and she would amuse and cheer up those who were in her company.

Soon people were delighted to be in her presence. Eventually she became a professional comedienne.

*   *   *

In November 1984, Galina Viltchinskaia was freed after five years in jail, which had been interrupted only by three months of freedom. From jail she went directly to a service of the underground Church in Habarovsk. It was the normal thing for her to do; after all, she had been imprisoned for her faith.

When she was released she was twenty-seven years old. The church in Russia which told her story to the outside world said that she was extremely thin, and had shrunk so that she looked like a child of eleven. Her face was yellow; she had little hair left. It was an effort to try to smile.

Because of continuous starvation in prison, her body was unable to manufacture fat. It was reported that it might be months before she could eat normally – assuming that she remained free, which was considered very unlikely.

When a friend met her who had known her in the old days, she exclaimed, 'What have they done to you? You look like a child!'

Galina replied meekly, 'I should have made myself look like a child of God, but I suppose I did not, so they did it their own way.'

*   *   *

The Russian Baptist leader Mihail Khorev tells of one of his childhood experiences.

During the siege of Leningrad in 1941, he was living with his mother and three other small children (his father had died in jail for his faith in Jesus). The family was doomed to starvation.

His mother used to pray, 'Thank you, God, that you love us so much.' Little Mihail always wondered about that. *If God loves us so much, why can't we have a piece of bread?*

One day she brought home a piece of cheese, divided it into four, and left the room. Mihail wondered why there were not five pieces. Unsure what to do, he held his piece in his hand.

After a few minutes, his mother came back into the room and asked, 'Does anybody have a piece of cheese left?' Mihail nodded. His mother continued, 'Old Kolia, our neighbour, is dying of hunger. I asked him what was his last wish, and he said, "Something to eat". The last wish of a dying person ought to be granted. Would you give up your piece of cheese?'

Mihail went with his mother to see how Kolia would eat the cheese. When his mother placed it in the dying man's mouth, he smiled and breathed his last. He had not been able even to swallow the morsel.

Mihail was tempted to remove the cheese from the dead man's mouth and eat it himself. When would he ever see cheese again? His mother saw what was going on in his mind.

At last he said, 'I gave the cheese not to Kolia, but to God. I won't take back a sacrifice given to Him.'

His mother was happy. Later Khorev wrote, from the same jail in which his father had died, 'I can testify that the greatest happiness for a man is to be totally consecrated to God.'

Have we made vows to God which we have later regretted? Then let us remember the saints and the martyrs – not only those of old, but also those of today.

*   *   *

A poorly-clothed barefoot Egyptian child who was about ten years old pointed to the Nile. He told me, 'As a baby, Moses floated on that river in a basket. Princess Hatsheput saved the little boy, who then went on to save his people and to save mankind from much ignorance. I have nothing either – but nobody has saved me.'

Incredible things can result from the saving of a single child.

I told this story to an adult afterwards, who retorted, 'Nonsense! How do you know that the child you save won't turn out to be another Hitler?'

How cynical we become as we grow up! Children are much less inclined to indulge in such negative speculations.

* * *

A Moslem boy of thirteen heard a Christian extolling the sublime teaching of Jesus, that we must love our enemies and turn the other cheek when we are beaten.

He said to himself, *I'll test this teaching.* He slapped the Christian.

True to his convictions, the Christian wept silently, saying, 'I am weeping for you.'

Surprised, the Moslem boy asked to be shown what part of Scripture contained this strange command. He was shown the text in Matthew chapter 5, and after reading the chapter through he decided to live according to its precepts. But he could not break the habit of swearing, nor could he see any 'blessedness' in mourning and in being poor.

He consulted a wise Christian, who explained, 'The teachings of the Sermon on the Mount are not commandments given to men; no man could fulfil them. There has only ever been one life motivated by such love, and that was the life of Jesus Himself. Ask Him to come into your heart, and He will change you.'

The boy did so, and became a new person.

* * *

A five-year-old, who had been ill since birth and had an incurable handicap, awoke from what the doctors had believed to be a coma.

He said to his parents, 'I saw Jesus. He sent me back. He did not tell me why.'

Many of us have escaped near-brushes with death. Let us believe that it was Jesus who sent us back. We might not know for what specific purpose, but it was surely so that we might serve Him whole-heartedly.

*   *   *

Mihai was eight years old when he came home from his Catholic school and announced that he was not going to pray any more.

I said, 'All right, you have the freedom to decide what you want to do. But can I ask you how you came to make such a decision?'

He complained that he had had two discouraging religious experiences that day.

In class, he had discovered that he had forgotten the exercise book that contained his homework. So he had prayed to God, who can do anything, to make the exercise book fly the short distance from home to school. Had I not told him that God took a whole man, Ezekiel, and transported him from Babylon to Tel-Aviv? So it would be no problem for God to fetch his exercise book.

The prayer had been in vain. The book did not arrive, and his teacher had scolded him.

Later, in the religious knowledge class, his teacher – a monk – told the pupils about a mason who swore at the virgin Mary while working on a high scaffold. As punishment, the blessed virgin allowed him to fall from the scaffold that very day and break his legs.

Unable to bear this, Mihai had stood up and said, 'Teacher, that can't be right. If someone wrongs my father, he forgives him. Surely the virgin Mary is even better than my father? If somebody speaks badly of her, surely she forgives. The man must have fallen because he was careless.'

In answer to this argument the teacher had given Mihai a slap.

We decided that the best course was to leave Mihai alone. We did not force him to pray.

At the same time I told his story to a lady who knew the Catholic archbishop, who made the monk apologise to Mihai. After that they became friends, and once more Mihai joined with us in prayer.

Later still, I shared a cell with that same monk in prison.

* * *

Political circumstances forced the father of Laura del Carmen Vicuna to flee from Santiago, the capital of Chile. She was still a baby when he fled. Soon afterwards he died, leaving the poor mother to work as a seamstress to support her two little children.

The mother, who was very beautiful, soon became the prey of a rich but brutal landlord, Manuel Mora. He grew tired of the woman he had lived with for a while, branded her like an animal with a red-hot iron, and chased her away.

The knowledge that her mother was living in sin with Mora caused the young Laura much suffering.

At the age of ten she took her first communion. On that day, in 1901, she wrote down the following resolutions:

1. My God, I wish to love and serve You all my life long. Therefore I give You my soul, my heart, myself.
2. I would rather die than insult You by sinning. Therefore I wish to shun everything that could separate me from You.
3. I take it as my aim to do everything I can to ensure that You may be known and loved, and to repair the insults that You receive daily from men, especially from my relatives.

When she was twelve, Laura unwittingly aroused the
lust of the same Mora and had to flee. To avenge this
insult, Mora bound her mother to a pole and flogged her
almost to a pulp. Laura, inspired by Jesus' words about
the good shepherd who gives his life for his sheep,
decided to offer her life to God on behalf of her poor
mother.

Soon she fell fatally ill. But despite her sickness, Mora
attempted to seduce her. Only the intervention of neighbours saved her.

Towards the end of her short life, she said to her
mother, 'I am dying. I have asked Jesus for this. For two
years I have offered my life to Him so that He might give
you the grace of repentance. Mother, before I die, will I
have the joy of knowing that you will return to God?'

Her mother promised, and Laura died breathing the
words 'Thank you, Jesus. I die satisfied.'

She was thirteen.

Her mother kept her promise and became a believer.
She refused Mora's demands, even when he threatened
her with a revolver.

Jesus wants more children like this, to offer their lives
for the salvation of sinners.

*   *   *

A child was anxious to wear spectacles, because he
thought they would give him the same prestige as his
father, who was a bespectacled executive.

He was taken to an optician, who showed him a chart
and asked what letters he could distinguish.

'I can see the first letters very well – H, I, C. But I can't
see the next ones – S, A, B – at all.'

Our amusement at this story belies our own inclinations! When we read the Bible, we readily accept what fits
in with our own ambitions and preconceptions. But we
fail to see what does not agree with our own theories or
pet sins, because we want to see the world through
spectacles of our own choosing.

*   *   *

Solutions

"God doesn't wear shoes."

I have shouted many Hallelujahs in my time – but I never thought to hurl them at the enemy's head!

My grandson at the age of five was determined to become a soldier, though he was not sure whether in the American, Israeli, or Salvation army. He looked forward to the time when he would be able to shoot, but thoughtfully anticipated my reaction. 'Don't worry, Grandpa. I won't shoot with bullets – but with Hallelujahs.'

This struck me as being thoroughly biblical. Are praises to the Lord ('Hallelujahs') really as ineffective as we might imagine? In Joshua's time, when it was time for the Jews to capture Jericho, they were commanded not to shoot but to blow their trumpets and shout. A great victory was gained.

Consider too the great victory of Jehosophat over the Ammonites and Moabites – sworn enemies of the Lord –

when he sent an army of singers against them, praising the Lord. 'You will not need to fight this battle,' the Lord promised, and the enemy was utterly destroyed and left much booty.

We would do well to shoot with Hallelujahs!

* * *

I have always enjoyed telling Bible stories to my grandchildren. I remember telling Alex how Nebuchadnezzar king of Babylon had set before his citizens the alternative of bowing before a statue portraying him as a god, or being thrown into a burning fiery furnace.

I asked Alex what he would have done. 'Would you have bowed to another god than our heavenly Father?'

'No way!'

'So you would have let yourself be thrown alive into the fire?'

'No way!'

'What other choice would you have had?'

'I would have thrown Nebuchadnezzar into the fire!'

* * *

Five-year-old Alex listened carefully to Jesus' story of the man who owned a hundred sheep, lost one, and searched until he found it. Joyful at reclaiming his loss, he gathered his friends for a feast. The conclusion of the story is that in heaven 'there will be more joy over one repenting sinner than over ninety-nine people who need no repentance'.

'What did you learn from the story?' Alex's father asked him.

'The man should have watched over his sheep more carefully; then he would not have lost one.'

Clergy expend a great deal of energy on revivals and on seeking to rehabilitate Christians who have gone astray. Would it not be better to warn Christians about the pitfalls and bypaths that might lead them astray in the first place?

* * *

When he was four Mihai said to me, 'Father, what can I do? I'm bored.'

I suggested that he should think about God.

'What can I think about Him with my little mind? He can think about me with His big mind.'

Instead of theological speculations, which are often fruitless because of the limitations of our minds, we would do better to assure ourselves, through Christ, of God's friendship. Then He will be free to take care of us without hindrance.

*   *   *

A child tried to draw a picture of God, and was rebuked. 'Give up this silly attempt. Nobody knows what God is like.'

He answered simply. 'They will when I have finished.'

*   *   *

Whenever I came home after work, Mihai would ask, 'Father, did you bring me anything? Good evening.'

One morning I read to him the story of how Jesus chased the merchants from the temple, and I took the opportunity to draw a lesson from what we had read.

'You are a temple – but you also have merchants that must be chased out.'

'What merchants?' he asked.

'One merchant is in the habit of asking first what gift I have brought, and then offering me a greeting.' He acknowledged that this was true.

'You have a second merchant,' I added. 'You love Jesus because He promises you Paradise. Would you love Him if He had no Paradise to give? To love Him just for what you can get out of Him is mercenary.'

Mihai replied, 'You have to pretend that you don't know He can give you Paradise, and say to Him simply, "I love you." But deep down, we know what He can give.'

*   *   *

A father agreed to be a one-man audience for a drawing-room Nativity play produced by his four children.

One played Mary, another Joseph, and the third an angel bringing the good tidings. The fourth child presented herself: 'I am the three Magi who have come from the East.'

When it was pointed out that she could not possibly be *three* wise men, she replied, 'Why not?'

And why not, indeed? Nobody is a single self, but rather a cluster of selves. We have the outward man, the inner man, the hidden man of the heart, the Id, the Ego, the Super-Ego. Often we 'talk to ourselves', or conduct mental arguments with ourselves.

It was the best in Peter that acknowledged Christ as 'the Christ, the Son of the living God'. It was the worst in him that denied his Master, saying, 'I do not know the man.'

To a greater or lesser degree, we are all 'split personalities'. Very young children are probably the most integrated among us.

One child can play all three Magi. Were an adult to attempt the role, the three would probably quarrel within him.

* * *

A mother was putting her child to bed. 'Don't forget to pray for Grandma, that she might grow very old with us.'

'Why?' asked the child. 'Wouldn't it be better to pray that God will make her young again?'

The fact is, that those we pray for will one day be young again.

* * *

Andrew Carnegie, who was known as the King of Steel, became rich as the owner of the greatest steel mills in the world.

When he was a ten-year-old boy in Scotland, he had a rabbit-hutch but no food for his little animal friends. So he told the neighbourhood boys that if they would gather clover and dandelions for the rabbits, he would name the animals after them. The deal was accepted.

Carnegie learned early in life how fond men are of their own names, and he applied that knowledge throughout his life.

Years later he named his steel mill in Pittsburgh after Edgar Thomson, director of the Italian railway company to which he wanted to sell steel rails. He had learned his lesson well!

Perhaps he had been inspired by reading what the Bible says in this regard. God promised Abraham, 'I will make your name great' (Gen. 12:2). Jesus promised the overcomer, 'I . . . will acknowledge his name before my Father and his angels' (Rev. 3:5).

Don Pedro, king of Brazil, intended to build the first hospital in his country, but had no money. So he issued a decree promising to everyone who gave the sum of $10,000 the title of Baron; to those who gave $20,000 the title of Viscount; and to those who gave the sum of $40,000, the title of Duke.

Money began to pour in, and the hospital was built. When inauguration day came, the veil covering the plaque was drawn aside to reveal this inscription: 'This hospital has been donated by human pride to human misery.'

At some time or other, everyone suffers from frustration or a lack of self-confidence. Consequently most people – including ourselves – are not as we would like them to be, and so we must meet them on their own ground as we attempt to win them for the kingdom.

Little Andrew Carnegie made use of a form of recognition-award to accomplish what he wanted. Let us apply his tactics, by making sure that in our churches every individual counts and is highly regarded.

*   *   *

The Sunday school teacher rambled on and on about the great characters of the Bible, starting with Adam and Eve; after an hour he had only progressed as far as Jeremiah.

'Now comes Ezekiel,' he announced. 'Where should I place this great prophet?'

A girl answered promptly, 'He can have my place – I'm leaving!'

Worse things can befall a preacher who has not learned the skill of communicating the gospel in terse words!

* * *

Nauka i Religia, the chief atheist magazine of the USSR, tells of the life of some Christian families who fled to the tundra (treeless arctic plains) and the taiga (swampy forests) of Siberia, in order not to associate with the God-hating Communists. They were discovered by anthropologists, after living a solitary life for forty years.

The scientists recorded the following story about two children in the community.

When a dog died, one child said, 'Let's bury it and put a cross on its grave.'

The other said, 'It wouldn't be lawful; the dog wasn't baptised.'

'Then let's put a garland on the grave. The dog will see it from heaven and rejoice.'

* * *

The atheist Einstein was brought to believe in God by a very small child; none other than Yehudi Menuhin, who astounded the world at the age of six with his violin-playing.

Einstein was visiting Menuhin's father, a practising Jew. They discussed ideas about God, and Einstein explained why he did not believe in the existence of God.

Yehudi, the wonder child, overheard the discussion while playing with his toys, and interrupted. 'Mr. Professor, I will prove to you that God exists.'

Amused, Einstein asked, 'What is your proof?'

Yehudi took his little violin and began to play. Einstein listened in ecstasy. When the child finished, he asked Einstein, 'If there were no God, how could a child of six play music that delights thousands in concert halls?'

Einstein never again claimed disbelief in God.

*   *   *

A little girl was talking to her mother, who was busy in the kitchen. She was telling her the events of the day. When she had finished, her mother said, 'Now go and polish Daddy's shoes.'

The girl did not enjoy the task, but she obeyed. Soon her father came in, but before he had a chance to thank her, she asked, 'Who polishes God's shoes?'

Her father was no theologian. Even if he had been, would his theological qualifications have been any help?

Somewhat embarrassed, he said, 'I suppose some good angel considers it an honour to do so.'

She was not satisfied. 'I was wrong – God doesn't wear shoes. He told Moses, "Take your shoes off, because you are on holy ground." God is always on holy ground in heaven. So He can't wear shoes, and there's no need to worry about it.'

At family prayers that evening, her father read how Jesus washed His disciples' feet.

She remarked, 'Jesus too had walked barefoot, or with just sandals, on the dusty roads of Palestine. It would have been nice if one of the disciples, after having his feet washed by Jesus, had offered to wash His feet. How come it didn't occur to any of them?'

Again, the father had no answer. He had never realised that we must not only accept Jesus' services, but also ask ourselves what little things we can do to help Him.

His daughter was wise beyond her years. It is important for us to consider the theology of children.

*   *   *

Today's headlines contain many unnerving and tragic events, among them the abduction, kidnapping, rape and murder of little children. Like many concerned parents, my son instructed both his children never to get into a stranger's car and to refuse any toys, sweets or money from strangers, however pleasant they may seem.

Once he decided to test Amelie. 'Would you go into someone's car if he offered you 500 dollars?'

'No way!'

'What if he offered you 5,000 dollars?'

'No way!'

'But what if he offered 50,000?'

'Well . . . 50,000 dollars is a lot of money. I'd tell him, "Give me the money and I'll ask my Daddy what I should do."'

Everyone has a breaking point. Anyone can resist a small temptation. But if it is really enticing or overwhelming – don't be in a hurry to give in. Rather, ask the One who has told you not to yield, the One on whose good intentions you can always rely.

*   *   *

A little girl in a wretched attic, whose sick mother had nothing to eat, knelt down by her bedside and said slowly, 'Give us this day our daily bread.' Then she went into the street, wondering where God kept His bread. Turning a corner, she spotted a large, prosperous bakery and thought, 'This must be the place!' So she went in confidently and said to the baker, 'I've come for it.'

'Come for what?'

'My daily bread,' she said, pointing to the tempting loaves. 'I'll take two, if you please – one for my mother and one for me.'

The baker wrapped them and gave them to his little customer, who started at once for the door.

'Stop, you little rascal!' said the baker roughly. 'Where's your money?'

'I haven't got any,' she replied simply.

'Haven't any? You little thief! What brought you here, then?'

The harsh words frightened the little girl and she burst into tears. 'Mother is sick, and I'm so hungry. In my prayers I said, "Give us this day our daily bread," and then I thought God meant me to fetch it, so I came.'

The rough but kindly baker was softened by the child's simple story, and instead of punishing her he said, 'You poor girl! Here, take this to your mother.' And he filled a large basket with bread and gave it to her.

*   *   *

The famous missionary to Africa, George Moffat, went to a new tribe and found to his amazement an inscription on a tree: 'The Christian school gathers here.' He did not know of any Christian missionaries who had been there before him.

Soon he found a twelve-year-old girl and asked her about the school. Well, she said, she was the head-mistress and the only teacher. She had lived in a neigh-bouring area for a time, where she heard the gospel; and she had returned to be the first missionary to the tribe.

It is not impossible to recruit children for home and foreign missions. In fact, children have special access to people's hearts.

*   *   *

A four-year-old boy from Sri Lanka, born with terrible deformities, listened intently as his father read in the Scriptures of how the disciples questioned Jesus about a man handicapped from birth: 'Who sinned, this man or his parents, that he was born blind?' (John 9:2).

The little boy broke in to ask, 'Mummy and Daddy, did you sin, and was I born blind because of that?'

The parents replied, 'We were God-fearing from child-hood. We are not conscious of any sin that would have deserved such punishment.'

The child then said, 'If that is so, I can be quiet. God will show in me some work of His.'

Now some thirty years later he is still alive, living mostly in hospitals in great suffering. Through his quiet witness, God shows that a cross can be borne patiently, lovingly, and with the hope of a better life in Paradise.

* * *

A boy of twelve threw a stone that accidentally hit one of the family geese on the head, killing it. Scared of the consequences of his carelessness, he buried the dead fowl, thinking that his mother would not miss it since they had a number of geese.

That evening his sister blackmailed him. 'Tonight you can wash the dishes. Otherwise I'll tell Mother what you did.'

So he washed the dishes. But when she tried to blackmail him again the next day, he replied 'No, today you wash the dishes. I told Mum all about it – and she forgave me.'

If you have committed a sin, however large, will you allow men and devils to inveigle you into more and more sins to cover up for the first? Better be quick to confess your sin to God. You will not surprise Him, for you are certainly not the first sinner. In fact, He would be surprised if you did not sin.

Know also, He forgives gladly. Where appropriate, confess your sin to the one you have wronged. And be aware how important it is that you do not let anyone force you into a wrong direction for ever, simply because you have taken a single step in that direction.

* * *

Admonitions

"Have one, child."

Origen, one of the most celebrated teachers of the ancient Church, passed through the gamut of suffering, though he did not attain to the privilege of dying a martyr's death.

He was only a child when his father Leonid (who later died for his faith) was arrested. When he heard that his father had been imprisoned, he did all he could to get himself jailed. His mother tried in vain to dissuade him. Finally she hid his clothes in desperation, and so forced him to stay at home.

Unable to do anything else, he wrote to his father: 'Beware of altering for our sake your decision, that you will suffer for Christ.'

Some Christians, thinking of the suffering that their loyalty to Christ brings their families, crack under pressures and persecution. Some are concerned lest their dangerous stand for Christ might make members of their family forsake the faith, because of the heavy burden that their father's sacrifice imposes on them.

I have heard many martyrs' children exclaim, 'If only my father had kept silent, my childhood would not have been so bitter.'

It is a great encouragement to have children like Origen. When I was in jail, my son who was then very young sent me letters in the same spirit in which Origen wrote. His first words to me, when he was allowed to see me after four years of detention, were: 'I have a rich Father who is taking care of me. You need not worry.'

The guards who were listening knew that he was my son. They wondered who this rich father might be.

May we encourage all who walk the way of the cross, assuring them that we do not resent the suffering that we may endure on their account. They should know that we are proud of them.

*   *   *

Strolling through a park with six-year-old Mihai and his friend, I sometimes found myself left behind as the boys skipped ahead. All of a sudden Mihai spotted a man reading a book. He went up to him and said, 'You'd be better reading the Bible!'

'Why?'

'It tells you how to go to heaven. If you don't, you will burn in hell. See that tall man over there? He's my father. He'll explain things better.' With such an introduction, I was able to take the opportunity to explain further. The man was won for God, and is today one of Rumania's greatest Christian poets.

Let us be evangelists, preparing the way like John the Baptist.

*   *   *

At five, Mihai attended a prayer meeting where there were prayers for the poor. 'Father,' he enquired, 'why do you bother God with prayers for the poor? Put your hand in your pocket and give!'

Many say that they do not know how to pray. A child provided the answer: a good deed is a wonderful prayer.

*   *   *

Once I explained to a child how tiny we are in this immense universe. Man ought to be humble. He is no more than a pebble.

The child (who was eight) replied, 'A pebble is a big thing. If it gets into the shell of an oyster, it becomes a pearl! It's wrong to despise oneself.'

When my granddaughter was seven, she watched me drawing men's faces. My drawing is worse than poor. She said earnestly, 'Grandpa, you are sinning. God made men to be beautiful. In your drawing you are making them ugly!'

I would have liked Picasso to have heard those words. He painted men ugly. But then I realised how often I have labelled people bad whom God loves and who are appreciated in His sight. A pebble can become precious, and a sinner can be of great value.

*   *   *

A five-year-old child was watching his mother as she made some cakes. Eventually he had a bright idea.

'Mummy,' he said, 'you have taught me so many nice words. May I teach you some as well?'

'Yes, of course. What would you like to teach me to say?'

'Try "Have one, my dear child!"'

The mother accepted the instruction immediately.

*   *   *

A group of us were discussing some serious mission problems. Amelie, who was about six years old at the time, was playing with her toys. Presently she interrupted. 'Grandpa, whereabouts is the word "problem" found in the Bible?'

'Nowhere that I know of.'

'But you all believe in the Bible – why are you so worried about something that's so unimportant, it isn't even mentioned in the Bible?'

I learned from this childish comment that looking for solutions to problems can be a useless exercise. It is simpler to reject problems, as things that do not belong to our lives.

In a life which has seen a great deal of suffering, I have learned that it is a sin to be plagued with headaches!

In the Bible, Jesus is called the head of the Church, and the believers are the body. Now, neither the foot nor the elbow can have headaches – only the head. So a believer with a headache has usurped the role of Jesus! It is as if he said, 'Come down from the throne! I am the head now. To prove it, I have headaches.'

In what sense do we have headaches like this?

At night Luther used to pray, 'God, is it my world – or Your world? Is it my Church – or Your Church? If it is Your Church and Your world, please take care of them. I am tired, I have to go to bed. Goodnight, my God. We will see each other in the morning.'

Let us leave everything in God's hands.

* * *

A boy of six overheard his older sister exclaim several times, 'Oh God!' Finally he said to her, 'You're doing wrong. Don't bother God.'

There is an old teaching in the Bible that is almost completely neglected. Jairus was rebuked: 'Why bother the teacher?' (Mark 5:35). The Psalmist says, 'My soul waiteth upon God' (Psa. 62:1, AV).

It is said that Teresa of Lisieux once chided a nun for constantly complaining about her troubles. 'Don't bother your sisters. They each have their own burdens.'

The nun accepted the rebuke in a good spirit. 'You are

right. From now on, I will only tell my troubles to Jesus.'

'Oh, no,' Teresa said, 'to Him least of all! Has He not suffered enough? Let Him have peace.'

* * *

A couple had always put their toddler in the church crèche, which is often very noisy. The day came when they decided to take him into the adult service for the first time. Before they did so, they told him, 'No talking in church'.

Everything went well while the choir was singing. But when the pastor began to preach, the boy shouted, 'No talking in church!'

Most older children would probably agree that there is too much talking in church! If the words they heard there were warm with love and truth – the 'real thing' (which is the meaning of the Hebrew word for 'word') – children would not mind long services. In the underground Church and in India, I have seen children quiet and interested in services lasting two to three hours.

* * *

When the Union forces finally gained victory in America's tragic Civil War, a jubilant crowd cheered Abraham Lincoln. He asked the people what should be done with the leaders of the rebellious South. They roared, 'Hang them!'

Lincoln's son, Tad, said, 'Father, don't hang them, but hang on to them.'

'You are right,' said his father, and acted accordingly; and so, in the opinion of some, made his assassination inevitable.

Whether the child reflected the man or the man the child, the Union was saved, and today America is one nation under God.

* * *

An American pastor was once asked to preach in Japan. When he came home, his young son asked him, 'How could people understand you? You don't speak Japanese.'

His father explained. 'I spoke a couple of sentences in English, then someone translated my words into Japanese.'

The child considered the explanation, and then said brightly, 'Father, why don't you stop in your sermons occasionally, and have somebody explain what they mean?'

*   *   *

In Aria, which is 50 kilometres west of Addis Ababa in Ethiopia, the first German missionaries bred cattle. They had a twelve-year-old boy looking after their herd.

One evening they observed him reading to his friends from the New Testament which they had translated. With great difficulty he stumbled through the words, trying to make some sense out of them. Finally, he closed the book and prayed: 'God in heaven, these white men have come to speak to us about Jesus, but they have heads like wood. They speak our language poorly and we can't understand them. Break open their heads, and put the words of our language into their brains, so that we can learn.'

Many good Christians who try to heed Jesus' advice to become as little children have difficulty in understanding some of the sermons for grown-ups. Preachers who can speak 'theologese' or 'philosophese' ought to learn to speak 'childese'. They would do well to remind themselves that their learned discourses are out of the reach of some listeners; or that their sermons are neither practical nor down-to-earth.

Jesus told us to feed His sheep – not His giraffes!

*   *   *

Once Amelie told a playmate, 'Tell your father not to ask my Grandpa to play chess. Grandpa hates to beat anyone even at chess, and he hates taking other people's pawns. I can see how he always loses at chess.'

I wish I were as altruistic as my grandchild perceives me to be!

*   *   *

Once we arrived at a hotel in San Francisco, and the manager informed us that we had no reservation and there were no rooms available. We argued with him, but it was no use. Finally Amelie spoke up. 'You're supposed to be saints. Why are you arguing? You should be praying.' Abashed, I bowed my head.

I had scarcely finished when the manager called me over, and said, 'You're in luck! I've found you a room.'

Amelie simply said, 'I hope you learned your lesson.'

I had. But would I remember it? Would she?

*   *   *

Sometimes when my son Mihai felt tired and prayed too briefly with his children, Amelie would pluck his sleeve and say, 'Daddy, we haven't prayed enough.'

Do we pray enough, by children's standards? We pray to the heavenly Father through Jesus. Does the holy Child think that we have prayed enough?

*   *   *

A group of thirteen-year-olds were asked to illustrate one of the Ten Commandments by drawing a picture. Several chose the seventh: 'You shall not commit adultery'.

One boy's effort showed a stick-man taking a stick-woman by the arm. Above his head was a wordless heart-shaped thought-balloon; above hers was a thought-balloon containing the question, 'What about my husband?'

When temptation blurs spiritual vision, it is helpful to focus attention on the possible effects of such a wrong course and to consider the likelihood of people getting hurt.

When the first atomic bomb was dropped on Hiroshima, the American pilot on his return was surrounded by reporters who asked, 'What do you think about this action?'

He replied, 'Why don't you ask the victims?'

The child in his rudimentary picture teaches us to put ourselves into the situation of the wronged party before we decide on a course of action that will cause that wrong.

* * *

Mihai was perhaps five years old when he sat on my lap and commented, 'You seem sad today. Why?'

I said, 'Because I realise I am a great sinner.'

He answered, 'You know what the proverb says: God takes away His gifts from those who are dissatisfied. Be thankful for what small goodness you have.'

At the same age, Amelie counselled me, 'Never complain about the state of your heart. You can be sure you will go to heaven, believe me.'

Cornelia, an eight-year-old, once interrupted one of my sermons. 'Don't tell lies when you preach! Don't say you are bad! Aren't you washed by the blood of Jesus? You are a saint!'

I was judging myself according to the deeds I had committed; these children believed my sermons asserting that those who trust in Jesus are made whiter than snow.

Why should Christians not be able to say, with David's simplicity, 'I am holy' (Psa. 86:2)? Indeed, we are called to be saints (1 Cor. 1:2).

* * *

A father told his child, with a wealth of detail, the parable of the lost sheep. To dramatise the story, he told how it had crawled through a hole in the fence at night and then wandered away. But fortunately the Good Shepherd was able to find it.

When his father finished, the child commented, 'I suppose Jesus made sure He mended that hole in the fence.'

Pastors too should concern themselves not only with regaining the backslidden, but with seeing to it that their parishioners do not backslide in the first place.

*   *   *

The late Archbishop Fulton Sheen once told about how he lost his way when trying to find Philadelphia Town Hall. He asked directions from a group of local boys. They told him the way and asked him why he wanted to go there.

'I have to give a lecture, on "The Way to Heaven",' he replied. 'Would you like to come with me?'

One boy laughed. 'How would you know the way to heaven, when you don't even know the way to the Town Hall?'

Children, like parents, are inclined to reject advice on how to get to heaven when their informant does not know how to behave decently upon earth.

The fact is that understanding and behaviour are not always cultivated to the same degree in a human being. David, and many other biblical and modern saints, could give very reliable information about the way to Paradise, while wandering far off from the paths of righteousness themselves.

Let us be sure that we discriminate between the man and his message. And for the clearest directions about the way to heaven, let us choose the Word of God.

*   *   *

A group of ten or so Christians of different persuasions were gathered in my home. We were having a heated debate about biblical problems.

The holy rule had been forgotten: that when discussion

waxes hot, it should be abandoned. People shouted at each other in anger.

Mihai, who was about four years old at the time, was present. When the argument reached a peak, he said four Greek words quietly: *'Kardia kai psyche mia.'*

The others, assuming he was speaking in tongues, asked me what they meant. I translated: 'One heart and one soul.' They were stunned into silence. The discussion ceased.

The only explanation I can offer is that Mihai must have heard me when I read the New Testament aloud in the original. The words occur in Acts 4:32: 'Now the multitudes of those who believed were of one heart and one soul.' I would have drawn my wife's attention to the beauty of the words, and the fact that they rhyme – kard*ia* . . . *mia*; and I would have explained to her what they meant.

Mihai had apparently remembered all this, and used the words at the right time.

Explanations

"I'm playing ball with God."

When Amelie was eight, she asked me to tell her yet again the story of how Jesus washed His disciples' feet. When I came to the words spoken to Peter – 'Unless I wash your feet, you have no part with Me' – she was very sad.

'Jesus didn't wash my feet; so I have no part with Him either,' she mourned.

I tried to explain. 'You were baptised. You have seen others being baptised.'

'But that's no help,' she countered. 'Jesus said that He must wash our feet. Anything else will not do.'

A chill travelled down my spine. I quoted many Bible verses before I found one that satisfied her completely: 'The blood of Christ cleanses us from all sins' – those of the head, the hands, the feet, 'just everything,' I explained.

'Well then,' she asked, 'if you are washed by Jesus, you are absolutely sure of entering heaven?'

'Absolutely sure.'

'Are you positive?'

'Yes, of course.'

'Then give me the names of the disciples whose feet He washed.'

I started to give her a few names. She broke in: 'Didn't He wash Judas' feet as well?'

'Yes, He did.'

'Then it is absolutely certain that Judas Iscariot is in Paradise.'

'I'm afraid not.'

'Why not?'

'Because he betrayed his Lord by selling Him for thirty pieces of silver.'

Amelie brought the discussion to an end by observing, with great candour and perception, 'Grandpa, it's not enough to be washed by Jesus; you have to behave afterwards.'

In that one sentence, she had summed up the entire epistle of James.

* * *

A Catholic child of eight gave a good explanation of 'holiness': 'Every person has a circle round his head, just as we see in the holy images. Some walk carefully so as to be right under the circle. Then it lights up. They are the saints. As for the rest of us, the circle remains invisible.'

No saint could have explained it better.

*   *   *

Nina and her small brother were fascinated by the siren of a passing ambulance.

Attempting to educate the wide-eyed toddler, Nina explained, 'They have the siren so that cars will stop and let them go past.'

Her brother disagreed. 'I don't think so. They make a big noise so that everybody will know "Here is somebody you should pray for because he's in great need."'

Who was right? I suspect both were!

*   *   *

I once read to Mihai from 1 Corinthians 11:28 – 'Let a man examine himself'.

Puzzled, he asked, 'How?'

I said, 'We must knock on our chests and ask, "Heart, do you love? Heart, do you love?"' To illustrate, I smote myself hard on the chest.

Mihai objected. 'In the railway station, I saw a man going from one train wheel to another, striking them with a hammer. I asked him to let me do it. When he handed me the hammer, I was surprised to see how light it was. He explained that if the wheels were struck with a heavy hammer at every station, they would eventually break.' (What Mihai had seen, of course, was the process of testing wheels for damage by listening to the vibrations of the metal when struck.)

'So,' continued Mihai, 'I believe we ought not to beat too hard on our chests, but only very lightly. Otherwise we might break our hearts! We should ask the heart very gently, "Do you love?" and if the heart whispers "Yes," we ought to be content.'

I learned something valuable that day. Self-examination, yes; but not self-torture.

*   *   *

Kindergarten children often surprise us with their un-expected juxtapositions of ideas. Looking at a picture-book about Africa, a five-year-old concluded, 'There must have been a lot of ice in the Sahara, and a lot of people must have slipped and fallen over – or God wouldn't have put so much sand on it!'

Can we fault this child, for trying to make sense out of a world for which the Father cares so deeply?

*   *   *

A rabbi walking down the street saw a little child playing with a ball. He fell into conversation with him.

'What are you doing?'

The boy replied, 'I'm playing ball with God.'

The rabbi laughed. 'How do you do that?'

The little one replied, 'I throw the ball up to Him, and He throws it back down to me.'

We should strive, like little children, to interpret events like these with such simplicity. Things do not fall because of the Law of Gravity, but because God allows them to fall for our good. He may use the Law of Gravity, which He ordained, to accomplish His ends; but we should see His hand in all that happens to us.

We interact with a living God, our loving Father; not with blind laws that impinge upon our material, psycho-logical or spiritual world.

*   *   *

A father gave pocket-money to each of his children, and asked how much of it they were going to give to Jesus. The youngest replied, 'Nothing'.

Surprised, the father queried, 'Don't you want to show Jesus how much you love Him?'

'I don't have to show Him a thing,' the toddler said earnestly. 'He knows exactly how much I love Him, even if I don't put a penny in the basket.'

The child was quite right. We must learn not to use religious jargon when we speak to children. To show

Jesus we love Him, we give ourselves. Then because we have given ourselves, we delight in giving things. God doesn't need our money – the cattle on a thousand hills are His – but He allows us the pleasure and privilege of filling human need by sharing with others.

*   *   *

Sometimes children display a refreshing honesty.

When Mrs. Booth of The Salvation Army preached on one occasion, she noticed a child in the front row crying. She paused to comment, 'I am moved to see a child weeping at the sufferings of Jesus.'

An adult might have been happy to accept the compliment. But the child stood up and admitted, 'No, lady; an insect got into my eye.'

Let us not pretend to have more spirituality than we actually possess!

*   *   *

Bramwell Booth was the General of The Salvation Army. His young children prayed, 'Dear Lord, send the Army a lot of money to make Papa happy.'

Alex says of his father, 'He wants to be a millionaire so he can give all the money to the Church.'

It is not money, but the love of money that is the root of all evil.

*   *   *

Children make theological mistakes just as adults do. A pastor once delivered a rousing sermon about sin and hell.

'One thing is certain,' he thundered. 'Every man, woman and child in this parish will die one day. There is no escape!'

A boy in the front row began to giggle.

'Every person in this parish,' reiterated the pastor, 'will die.'

The boy continued to laugh.

Affronted, the pastor challenged him. 'Why are you laughing?'

'I'm not from this parish,' he replied.

* * *

Amelie at the age of five volunteered her own explanation as to why the capital of Rumania is called Bucharest.

'It's because the country is Communist, and if you're caught with a religious *book*, *arrest* will follow.'

* * *

In a small provincial town in Rumania I went to the Presbyterian church and asked for the pastor. Some children were playing in the churchyard and one of them, who was about twelve years old, offered to take me to the manse.

As we walked, I asked him about himself and learned that he was to be confirmed the next week. I asked him, 'Do you believe in Christ?'

He replied determinedly, 'Oh, no. I'm only getting confirmed because my mother really insists.'

'Why do you feel like that?'

His answer was remarkable. 'I believe that if it were true that God created, 2,000 years ago, the marvellous Christ I'm taught about, He would also have made some little Christ in every generation, in every town, to show us that such a character is possible. But – I've never met a Christ. My father is dead, my mother is poor and has lots of children. Nobody has ever given me a sweet or shown me any kindness. There never was a Christ.'

I asked another question: 'Isn't your pastor a little Christ?'

'No,' he said.

We had arrived at the pastor's house. The boy left. I took the opportunity of relating to the pastor what the child had said, emphasising his desire to meet a little Christ.

'What an idiot!' said the pastor.

He was right. But who was the idiot?

*   *   *

Little children love stories. When Amelie was five she begged, 'Grandpa, please tell me about Jesus, but every little bit, from when He was born to the very end.' Then she added, 'I know you can't do that. Nobody can tell the whole story of Jesus because it isn't finished yet.'

And so it is written in Mark 1:1 that the evangelist records only 'the beginning of the gospel about Jesus Christ.'

Let us also acknowledge that we know very, very little; but the little we do know is so beautiful that it is well worth repeating and well worth investigating further.

*   *   *

I remember having to tell Mihai off for some wrongdoing when he was small. Convicted, he stood before me with bowed head. I asked him, 'Why don't you look me in the face?'

'I don't want to look at your mouth when it says harsh words,' he said simply. 'I want to look at the loving heart from which they come.'

*   *   *

A child was taken to the opera for the first time. He saw *The Masked Ball* and was very impressed.

At home, he said to his father, 'I didn't understand what was happening on stage. What is the opera about?'

His father replied, 'It is all sung in Italian, and I don't understand Italian. But the orchestra conductor's son is in your class at school. When you are at his house, why not ask his father? I'm sure he'll be glad to explain.'

The boy did so, but the conductor could not help. 'I have to spend my time seeing to it that every instrument and singer comes in at the right time. I've never actually watched what happens on stage, so I can't tell you. But wait a minute: the tenor who sings the leading role will be here for tea soon. He'll explain everything.'

So the boy asked the tenor, but he replied, 'I'm not on stage all the time, and I've had to memorise so many roles. . . . I really don't care about what the others are singing while I get a bit of rest in my dressing room. But look, here is the stage manager. He'll tell you.'

The stage manager had little more to offer. 'I only have a very general idea. My concern is the scenery, not the plot.'

So the boy went to the author of the libretto, who replied, 'I only wrote the words. I've wondered myself, sometimes, about the weird music that draws attention away from the words.'

He went to the composer, but he only said, '*The Masked Ball*? Who knows? As far as I'm concerned, the author could have made the Governor of Boston a Spanish cavalier. For me, the text was just an excuse for my own musical fantasies.'

The child went back to his father, much enlightened. 'Nobody knows a thing. We're all playing some little part in a drama we don't understand.'

So it is written in Scripture: 'The man who thinks he knows something does not yet know as he ought to know' (1 Cor. 8:2).

Love is the key to knowledge and to meaning.

*   *   *

When she was eleven, Amelie had to write an essay in school on the subject of capital punishment. In her efforts to gather all the arguments for and against she consulted many people, including me.

Six-year-old Alex listened for a while, then gave his unsolicited opinion: 'I am for capital punishment – but with love.'

St. John of the Cross wrote, 'On the last day we will all be judged by love.' Sometimes life obliges us to use harsh methods and take up unpopular attitudes; but even these should be motivated by love.

*　　*　　*

The late Orthodox priest Sheludkov of Russia, a man much persecuted, tells in his book about a twelve-year-old boy in Moscow.

A terrible thing had happened; young Misha was a believer, and the Communist teachers had found out. A conclave of teachers gathered to persuade Misha to abandon his faith. They asked him, 'How can you believe in God? Have you ever seen Him?'

He answered, 'If I were to see Him, I would not believe in Him. The real God is invisible. Gagarin the first cosmonaut mocked Him saying, "I looked around in space and could see no God." Was he so ignorant? Didn't he know that God is invisible?'

We all wish sometimes that we could see God visible in our lives, giving direct answers to our questions or providing us with the things we most desire. But if He were thus visible, He would not be God. In our sinful state, we cannot look on Him and live. That is why God is the Invisible in the events of our lives, the mysterious, the awe-inspiring in our experiences.

We are pilgrims, bound for another world. What our senses can perceive in this world will never satisfy the human soul. We are looking for a better city, 'whose builder and maker is God'.

Then we shall see our Redeemer face to face, and know who He is.

*　　*　　*

The writer Elie Wiesel was once an inmate of a Nazi concentration camp. He tells of a starving Jewish child who was hanged for stealing a piece of bread.

The child asked for no explanation. He did not cry, nor even protest. Life had been given him without explanation, and in a cruel way, life was taken from him without explanation.

Where was God?

God was right there, on the gallows with the child, silent and hurting. What is there to say, in the solemnity of such an hour?

Christ too was 'led like a lamb to the slaughter . . . He did not open His mouth' (Isa. 53:7).

* * *

I explained to a child of nine that hatred is an evil.

She said, 'Then hate is sin, and so is love.'

'Where did you get the idea that love is sinful?'

'Well,' she said, 'Jesus said we should love each other as He loves us. Everything less is sin. I don't love anybody as Jesus does. I would not die on a cross for anybody.'

From this discussion I held on to the concept that to love less than Jesus does is sin.

On the altar of sacrifice in the temple of Jerusalem, the blood of animals was to be found, that cleansed worshippers from their trespasses. But once a year, the altar itself had to be cleaned.

Before God, even our good deeds are like filthy rags. Only Jesus' righteousness satisfies. Only His love is worthy of this name.

* * *

One evening the son of a celebrated evangelist threw a tantrum. When his mother went to sort him out, she asked him why he had behaved so badly.

'I didn't do it,' he said. 'The devil did it.'

Oh, that we would have the wisdom not to attribute to ourselves actions that we deplore, and not to despair when we fall into sin! The devil really does seek constantly to ensnare us in attitudes and actions that are alien to our nature.

Let us place the blame where it belongs, and quietly

acknowledge the mis-steps in our lives, and firmly denounce the devil's doings in our lives.

And then let us pray: 'Our Father . . . . lead us not into temptation, but deliver us from evil.'

* * *

A boy was making a brave attempt to draw a dog in pen and ink. The result was pleasing, except that the dog had no tail.

Naturally, an adult who saw the picture asked, 'Where's his tail?'

He answered disingenuously, 'It's still in the ink-bottle.'

Sometimes we are criticised for not being polished saints. A few years ago, there was a saying that was popular: 'Be patient with me – God isn't finished with me yet.'

Our virtues are still 'in the bottle', along with His promises.

'He who began a good work in you will carry it on to completion until the day of Christ Jesus' (Phil. 1:6).

* * *

A child asked his mother how he was born. She told him, 'God sent you into the world.'

'And how were *you* born?'

'I was sent by God too.'

'And Grandmother?'

'Yes, she was sent by God as well.'

'Mummy, why has there been no sex for such a long time in our family?'

In these days of television and *Playboy* Magazine, children are aware of sex from a fragile age. They won't stand for fables.

They should be told about sex, but told of it in its fullness – its beauty and its dangers. They should know that God has provided a framework for the precious gift of life to appear.

* * *

A child came back from Sunday School very excited. 'We learned how Moses brought the Jewish people over the Red Sea!' he told his mother. 'He just waved his stick, and building materials fell from heaven! Then he waved it again, and everything stuck together and made a huge bridge! Then he waved his stick again – and there were horses and carts to carry the old people!'

His mother frowned. 'I'm sure he can't have said that.'

'Well,' replied the child, 'if I told what he *really* said – you wouldn't believe it!'

Nowadays children suck scepticism with their mother's milk. They don't take Bible stories on trust.

We must not only tell children the stories of God's miracles. We must also explain to them that an almighty God can do things we cannot; and we must explain to them why God worked miracles, and how trustworthy is His Word.

* * *

Epilogue

Love for God should always
resemble that of a child.

Not long ago, I had a dream that made a vivid impression
upon me.

I was in a prison cell again. On my bed was a giant
caterpillar. I wanted to get rid of it, but couldn't because
the door was locked. I had no alternative but to kill it, and
I succeeded in doing so only after great efforts. Ex-
hausted from my exertions, I suddenly realised that what
I had killed was the child in me – that capacity to believe
wholeheartedly, love unstintingly, trust implicitly. I had
killed the best in me.

I awoke with a feeling of great sorrow. Is it possible to kill the child within the man?

Today, abortion is a controversial issue. Some fifteen millions of the unborn have been killed in the United States alone during the last decade. In Red China, new-born girls are slaughtered by the thousand, because women are not allowed to have more than one child and they would rather have a boy.

We also kill spiritually. We murder the child within, the child who, as Nietzsche wrote, 'wishes to play'. Even Marx, that implacable foe of religion, was driven to admit: 'I have to concede to Christianity one great merit. It has taught men to love children.' It has done more than that. It has taught men to love the child in themselves.

In this area, children's theology is unique.

After Christ had ascended to heaven, His followers referred to Him as 'the holy child, Jesus' (Acts 4:27, AV). Why?

A Cambodian girl, Arn Chorn, who grew up in the middle of the holocaust that annihilated at least two million of her countrymen – including her family – gives an interesting answer.

Children are less angry than adults and forget insults more quickly. Maybe children know more about their imperfections, and when we do, we have a chance to laugh at ourselves more easily and not take ourselves so seriously. Maybe as children, we can feel a brother-hood of imperfection. Children are less sure that they are absolutely right. Adults, who are sure that they *are* absolutely right make war – even religious war – over their absolute rightness.

Jesus chides us with the observation, 'You have forsaken your first love' (Rev. 2:4) – a child's love. Love for God should always resemble that of a child.

Many believe that the innocence of children is a myth

created by adults. Freud went so far as to call children 'polymorph perverse'.

I do not wonder. He was repeating what David said long ago: 'Even from birth the wicked go astray; from the womb they are wayward and speak lies. Their venom is like the venom of a snake' (Psa. 58:3–4).

This is the bitter complaint of a father who had several wicked children. Perhaps Freud experienced similar frustration.

As for Jesus, He admired in little children their unqualified love, trust and openness. When the religious leaders and theologians of the day shut Him out, the little ones, with their children's theology, accepted Him, climbing all over Him, and, I think, hugging and kissing Him with unabashed warmth and ardour. Without knowing theology, they embraced the God about whom theologians argue.

The heart of the gospel – the Good News to which all Scripture testifies – is that God loves, forgives and accepts His creatures; and Jesus came as Man to demonstrate this true character of Deity (cf. John 3:16).

May God grant us the grace to grasp this, with the simple faith of a child!

*   *   *

The author welcomes correspondence. You may write to him at:

Christian Mission to the Communist World
PO Box 19
Bromley
Kent
BR1 1DJ

Who Speaks For God?

Charles Colson

In a day when the Christian gospel is mocked, when moral absolutes are denied, when evil is rampant and even welcomed, God calls his people to speak bravely on his behalf. The issue of power, AIDS, capital punishment, the trivialisation of sin, secularisation (particularly within the Church), and the disastrous divide between personal piety and public action are all examined by the former aide to President Nixon in this cogent and challenging book on confronting the world with real Christianity.

'He combines a clear, attractive style, the sharpness and precision of a top lawyer, the breadth of vision of a statesman, with pungent biblical perspectives.' *Church Times*

'Thought-provoking reading to dip into and mull over.' *Christian Family*

One Heart, One Voice

Andrew Maries

What exactly is worship? And what part does music play in its expression? Should every church have a choir? What about structure – does it impede spontaneity?

These and other questions are explored in this practical and challenging book on the ministry and mission of music in worship. With a foreword by Betty Pulkingham.

'Here is practical and sensitive help from someone with a classical music background, harnessed to an openness for the needs of today's church.' *Anne Watson*

'Every minister and church musician should buy it.' *Church of England Newspaper*

Andrew Maries worked closely with David Watson at St Michael-le-Belfrey in York.

Heaven On Your Doorstep

Max Sinclair

The family is under threat today as never before. Even Christians wonder whether God can make any difference when they hit problems.

Max Sinclair, author of bestseller *Halfway To Heaven*, has discovered from experience that God both sets the standards for family happiness, and provides the means whereby it can be achieved. Writing frankly about his romance with Sue, marriage, parenthood, God's call to full-time Christian work and the serious car accident which left him partially paralysed, Max demonstrates that the miracle of happier relationships is within the grasp of every Christian.